naked
28 days

Rahima —
I hope you know
how beautiful you always!
XO Heather

naked
28 days

your guide to living smarter, feeling sexier, and loving your body

by heather esposito

MS, CHHC, Chef,
Body Code Practitioner

Copyright © 2016 Heather Esposito

All Rights Reserved. No part of this publication may be reproduced in any form or by any means, including scanning, photocopying, or otherwise without prior written permission of the copyright holder.

We diminish our holiness by being obsessed with what's wrong instead of finding what's right. We criticize ourselves to the point that we forget about who we are and the greatness that is our bodies.

Ilyana Vanzant

dedicated to all of the women who have yet to
see how smart, sexy, and divine you are.

my desire is that this practice will open up
a new world for you and that you will impact
others with your vibrant energy.

acknowledgments

I would maintain that thanks are the highest form of thought, and that gratitude is happiness doubled by wonder.

G. K. Chesterton

I have never considered myself a writer. I'd go so far to say that I don't particularly enjoy writing. Yet, when you feel as if an idea has been handed to you and it seems as though it won't leave you alone until you do something about it, you get to work writing.

And then you stop writing. At least that's what I did. More often than not my mind seemed to be plagued with the thought, "you don't have anything worthwhile to say."

Fortunately, I have amazing friends who wouldn't let me believe that crappy story.

Joyce Rosenblum--you have always believed in me and have encouraged me to share my voice since the day we met. I'm grateful for our friendship and look forward to many more years!

Amy D--our friendship is the best take away from the conference where we met! Thank you for your support, encouragement, and telling me that I am a writer!

Alex Changho--despite your jokes, you are a great friend that I'm so glad I found. This book wouldn't be here if you didn't bring it to life through the cover and through you talking me off the ledge when I was literally ready to throw in the towel on everything. I know it makes you happy to know that you are helping women everywhere become smarter and sexier!

Paula-Glynn Hundertajlo-my dear friend. I am so grateful that you consistently give me space to be me. You are a gem.

Mark Logue--my favorite Irishman! Every conversation I have with you leaves me thinking, "Shit, I need more of him in my life!" You are a great friend and an amazing coach, and if it weren't for a phone call where you basically kicked my butt, I would have let this project fall to the wayside!

Elizabeth Ada Ramasamy--it takes someone special to be my coach and you have been doing the job beautifully. Thank you for your confidence, for not buying my stories, and for believing in me.

Beverly Wixon —I am so fortunate to have been introduced to you. Thank you for cleaning this up, understanding the direction I wanted this book to go and making it better than it started out!

Chris Schinke—every girl needs to have a "Chris" in their life. I am so grateful for you and our friendship. You make me shake my head & sigh often but even more, you make me laugh a lot. It takes a lot for me to do that—thank you!

Lea Newman—my sister from another mister. Thank you for always speaking to me in love, providing the "trash can" when I need to vent and not making me wrong for anything I am feeling.

Tony Robbins Coaching Team--"every dream grows with a team" and I would not be who I am today if it weren't for being a part of the Tony Robbins Coaching Team. Marc von Musser--your tireless efforts do not go in vain. Brenda Schinke--your femininity is such a gift to this team and I'm beyond grateful to know you.

table of contents

why 28 days naked?

the two words that change everything

how to use this book to get smarter & sexier

day 1 luxurious hair

day 2 eyes that shine

day 3 ears to hear

day 4 smiling mouth

day 5 powerful nose

day 6 cheekbones created from a genuine smile

day 7 keep your chin up

day 8 stick your neck out

day 9 i got your back

day 10 breasts --your natural jewels

day 11 receive with open arms

day 12 hands on

day 13 belly --the center of our spirit

day 14 our heart has answers

day 15 the brain that changes itself

day 16 hips don't lie

day 17 i love my thighs

day 18 on bended knee

day 19 sexy calves

day 20 jump in with both feet

day 21 comfortable in your own skin

day 22 shake your booty

day 23 feel in one's bones

day 24 powerful pancreas

day 25 happy, balanced kidneys

day 26 brilliant ovaries

day 27 vagina --a place of pleasure

day 28 lungs --breath of life

a smarter, sexier, happier, you

about the author

why 28 days naked?

Without exception, begin every day of your life with gratitude. As you look in the mirror, say, "Thank you, God, for life, for my body, for my family and loved ones, for this day, and for the opportunity to be of service. Thank you, thank you, thank you."

Dr. Wayne Dyer

A few years ago I was working as an intensive in-home therapist for kids that were either at risk of being removed from their homes or they had just returned to their homes after being in treatment centers. These kids were anywhere from 6 years old to 16 years old.

My client was the kid who was displaying behaviors that were causing stress in the family but my job entailed working with the whole family, as it is rarely the person who is acting out that is in need.

It was contracted that I spend approximately 10 hours a week with the family. As you can imagine, that is an intense amount of time (hence it being called "intensive in-home therapy").

Our sessions were generally 3.5 hours 3 times a week. During the sessions I'd work with the child-client individually for part of the time, then we would do a family session for the remaining time.
In one particular case, I was working with a 14-year-old girl who lived with her mother and stepfather who had a 1-year-old daughter together.

During the family session the parents were talking about how much they were fighting about various issues and they felt like there was no end to it.

As we discussed action steps to take before the next session, I gave them an assignment: whenever they fought, they had to fight in their room and they had to do it naked.

As soon as I said it the step-father said, "oh, that will never happen; she never lets me see her naked."

Internally my thought was "WHAT??? You are married! You just had a kid together. Why do you not want your husband to see you naked?"

Being the professional that I am, I calmly and compassionately asked the mom, "What's going on that you don't want him to see you naked?"

She proceeded to say that she doesn't like how she looks since she had the baby and is embarrassed by her body.

After our session was over, I couldn't stop thinking about the mom's comment and my inability to immediately help her. I later consulted with a colleague, a fellow health coach and asked her if she looked at herself naked daily. She said she did but that she had many friends and clients who said that they didn't because they were ashamed of how they looked.

This made me so sad.

Then I remembered a time about ten years ago when I was heavier than I am now and I always thought I was ugly—looking at myself naked or having anyone else look at me naked was not something I welcomed. I had a low-grade depression that never seem to go away and most of the time I didn't want to live (more about that in day 15).

That started me wondering about what changed in me to move me from hating my body to embracing and loving it?

In many ways I took myself through the process that you are about to go through. I allowed myself the opportunity to really look at my body--completely naked. As I looked with the intention of seeing if there was anything good about it, I gave myself the gift of seeing me for the first time.

Whether it was for my nose that I didn't like or my bloated belly, I began to express gratitude for the body I live in. As I started that practice, everything changed. I will admit though, it wasn't easy at first.

Really seeing myself naked allowed me the opportunity to get honest with myself. When I really saw and acknowledged that my arms didn't have the definition I desired, I decided to work to create the arms I did want. With each push up I expressed gratitude for having arms that worked.

Seeing my bumpy Italian nose confronted me with the thought of getting a nose job. Deciding that the pain of the surgery would be greater than the pleasure of having a different nose I decided my best option would be to choose to love the nose I was given, so I began to thank it for being the amazing gift it is. I thanked it for allowing me to smell the delicious aromas in my kitchen and for taking in air with each deep breath.

Looking at my stomach, I finally admitted to myself that I had become a bit overweight and that it was a bit more jiggly than I was comfortable with, so I decided to change my diet to support how I wanted to feel and look. As soon as I eliminated gluten from my diet, my flat stomach returned. With each bite of veggies, I thanked my stomach for processing the foods it needed to create health in my body.

There was no magic wand that made me love myself over night, but there was a magic wand that helped me increase my love for myself over time.

As I immersed my mind in the practice of gratitude I slowly began to feel the cloud lift from my mind. I started to see myself for who I really was, one who was, to quote Marianne Williamson, "born to make manifest the glory of God."

It wasn't that I changed; it was that the true and best version of myself was given permission to finally live.

The crazy thing is, that as I began the exercise of daily gratitude for my body, so many other areas of my life shifted—my health, my career, my relationships, and my spirituality.

I won't act as if I have a perfect life now because of the gratitude practice. There are definitely times that it takes everything in me to express gratitude for my body.

Just when I thought I had this almost mastered, my ability to stay in gratitude versus negativity towards my body was tested in a huge way.

This past year I decided to do something I had always wanted to do--I started taking Aerial silks classes. (If you don't know what this is, Google Aerial Silks. It is my absolute favorite workout—it's challenging, strength building, and beautiful—I highly recommend it if you are looking for something new and unique.)

Twice a year the school has a student showcase where the students perform a self-choreographed piece. Although I had only been taking classes for four and a half months, one of my instructors encouraged me to perform.

I thought she was crazy for suggesting it and happily thought that I would get out of it because I had a work trip scheduled during the weeks leading up to the show, which would cause me to miss a week of obligatory practice time.

A week and a half before auditions my work trip was pushed back a few months so I decided to audition, mainly because I knew that it would take me way out of my comfort zone and cause me to grow exponentially. I had barely enough time to choreograph a piece and practice before the audition AND I have NEVER done anything like this before—to say that I was nervous was an understatement.

I've never taken any dance class or gymnastics like so many of the other girls in the class, so I felt completely inadequate. My little, inner saboteurs started screaming in my mind, "Who do you think you are to do this? You aren't good enough! You aren't muscular enough, you aren't skinny enough! and your choreography is ridiculous!"

A few of my girlfriends literally had to talk me into going to the audition.

My inner voices became even louder when I found out I "passed" the audition and would be performing. *Crap! What did I get myself into?*

The inner voices became even louder again when I went shopping for a leotard for the performance. I'd gotten comfortable with looking at myself naked but looking at myself in a leotard was a whole different idea. Stepping into the Aerial studio in a leotard, looking at myself in the full mirror, seeing myself in a way I had not seen myself before was truly an exercise in practicing what I teach--gratitude.

As I looked at different parts of my body, the natural inclination was to berate myself. I had to very consciously choose to say and think thoughts such as, "Thank you for my belly for it houses muscles that allow me to do amazing moves on the silks; thank you for the cellulite on my legs as it protects my bones from breaking."

Hate and gratitude cannot co-exist; there is no room for hating our bodies when we express gratitude for them. In order to get back to a place of love of my body, gratitude was the only way.

There are times when expressing gratitude may come easy for you. There are times, such as what I'm experiencing as I write this, when it may be challenging. I can say with 100% certainty that my life is richer and has more meaning when I take back my power in how I experience life by choosing gratitude. And, I believe it will be the same for you.

My desire is that after these 28 days you feel smarter, sexier, and happier. My desire is that every time you look or think about your body, gratitude will be your first thought.

For the next 28 days I want to invite you on this journey with me.

- ♥ 28 days of being open to the magic of gratitude for your body.

- ♥ 28 days of experiencing shifts that you have been wanting.

- ♥ 28 days of seeing yourself with new eyes.
- ♥ 28 days of pure love.

Are you in?

If so, I welcome you on this journey.

I can't wait to hear about the shifts you make along your journey!

the two words that change everything

I started out giving thanks for small things, and the more thankful I became, the more my bounty increased. That's because what you focus on expands, and when you focus on the goodness in your life, you create more of it. Opportunities, relationships, even money flowed my way when I learned to be grateful no matter what happened in my life.

Oprah Winfrey

Why do I believe that a book on gratitude can help you become smarter, sexier, and happier?

Honestly, I don't think that reading this book—or any book for that matter will help you become smarter, sexier, and happier. What I do know to be true is that when you *practice* what is in the book you *will be* become smarter, sexier, and happier. When you use the two magic words "thank you," life changes.

What is it about gratitude and the words *thank you* that can bring about changes to how we experience our lives?
The lesson of how gratitude can change our experience of life was taught to me by two separate and different experiences.

When I was a teenager I volunteered at a rescue mission that fed dinner to the homeless. One particular evening, my best friend and I were assigned to the kitchen to help cook that evening's dinner of hot dogs and chili.

About 15 minutes before we were to serve dinner, the head cook, a very happy man who was formerly homeless, realized that we were short hot dog buns. Unsure of what to do, he left to talk to the director of the program. A few minutes later he returned with a gigantic smile on his face as he said, "Praise God, Hallelujah! Thank you, Jesus!"

Curious, we asked what he was so happy about. He proceeded to tell us that when he left the building a bakery truck pulled up to drop off their leftovers and they had the *exact* amount of hot dog buns we needed. I had never seen anyone so grateful for something as little as hot dog buns in my life.

Flash forward about ten years. I was on a boat in the Bahamas with a friend's brother for a scuba diving excursion. The water was crystal clear, the temperature was beyond perfect, and there was not a cloud in the sky. There was nothing about the day that wasn't dreamy and for many people the entire trip would have been a dream vacation.

Unlike the homeless guy, my friend's brother was what many would consider successful, as he had more financial wealth than many people could imagine.

Noticing the almost scowl on my friend's brother's face as we were heading to the first dive spot, I asked him if he was excited about this trip. Glumly he replied, "No, I've done so many things like this, nothing excites me."

Wow. What a difference in attitudes! A man who had experienced homelessness was incredibly grateful for something as simple as hot dog buns while another man who had never experienced any kind of financial struggle in his life expressed no gratitude for the experience of being able to go scuba diving from a boat on a beautiful day in the Bahamas. He had achieved so much financial success, yet he was not fulfilled.

The world's top Peak Performance Coach, Tony Robbins says, "Success without fulfillment is the ultimate failure" and that's all I could think that day on the boat.

What I learned that day was that it doesn't matter how much or little one has in life, if you aren't grateful for what IS in your life, then nothing will make you happy.

The same is true for our bodies. As women we often think thoughts such as, "if I was skinny, I'd be happy or if my _____ was different I'd be happy." Unfortunately, it doesn't work like that. If we are unhappy with what we've been given, it won't matter how gorgeous others believe we are, we will always feel unfulfilled.

I've counseled and coached hundreds of beautiful women who were miserable because they said, "If (fill in the blanks) was different I'd be happier." They couldn't grasp the fact that other women looked at them and say "If I just looked like her I'd be happy." We rarely see ourselves as others see us.

I've also counseled and coached women who may not have been what the world would call *beautiful*, but they were filled with vibrant energy because they lived lives full of gratitude.

What specifically can gratitude do for you? It can add much to your life, including, but not limited, to the following.

awareness

Gratitude will allow you to notice the things that you already have that, rather than on what you don't have. What we focus on, we feel—if we are focused on always finding what is wrong with our bodies, we will always find what is wrong.

If we focus on finding what's good, we find more of those things. The more things we find that are good, the happier we are.

We also become more in touch with the messages our body is sending us. As we become more in touch with the messages our body is sending us we begin to hear its subtleties and we are then able to give it what it needs to be its highest and best self.

inspiration

As you practice gratitude you will notice that your happiness increases. Happiness is naturally contagious to those whose paths you cross. Yes, there will be those who are determined to stay miserable, but for those who are looking for inspiration, you just may be that person for them.

legacy

Whether you have daughters or not, all women at some point in our lives have a younger female who looks up to us. It could be a niece, a neighborhood kid, or someone you mentor. Be an inspiration, instead of another negative woman in their lives.

We females are bombarded with the messages that we should "hate" our bodies. It is time for us to change that story to one where woman are in love with the bodies they have, and because of this love, they do everything they can to be in alignment with that. They take care of their bodies, feed them well, and live a lifestyle that supports their bodies.

By making this change, imagine how amazing you will feel when other women tell you that because of you, their life was changed?

perspective

There is a saying that "success breeds success," which basically means that when you celebrate your successes, you create more success. The same is true with gratitude. The more you express gratitude for what you have, the more you will find you have to be grateful for.

feel better physically

In a 2012 study published in the online journal *Personality and Individual Differences,* grateful people experienced feeling healthier than people who did not express gratitude. Grateful people were more likely to take care of their physical health by exercising more and eating more health supportive foods.

Based on this study, expressing gratitude can boost our immune systems, literally making us healthier.

feel better emotionally

Dopamine is considered the brain's primary *reward* chemical and it desires nothing more than attention. (We women can all relate to that, can't we?) When the brain feels rewarded, it releases dopamine. Our brains (and I believe our souls) then want to repeat the action that triggered the dopamine so it can trigger more dopamine so we can keep feeling good.

When we focus on good things and express gratitude for those things, even if the thing that we are expressing gratitude for is imaginary, the brain releases dopamine. (By the way, the brain does not know the difference between real and imaginary events.) Therefore, we actually have control over how we feel by choosing to think thoughts that will support us.

attractive

It is generally believed that people who are grateful tend to be more optimistic, are perceived as being nicer, they smile more, they are less self-centered, and they have greater levels of self-esteem. All of these qualities create a vibrant energy that automatically makes you to appear more attractive to anyone you come across.

my hope for you

Gratitude isn't only reserved for those who are *lucky* or *beautiful*. I'd suggest that people are *lucky* and *beautiful* because they are grateful for even the smallest things.

These two words, "thank" and "you" have such amazing power when they are combined into one simple phrase. The choice is yours to use them.

My desire for you is that at the end of the 28 days naked you will feel exponentially beautiful, you will see yourself in a new light, and you will experience life at a level you have yet to know.

how to use this book to get smarter and sexier

Knowledge is the treasure, but practice is the key to it.

Ibn Khaldoun Al Muqaddima

Congratulations!

If you've gotten this far, I know that you are a woman who wants to create the best possible version of yourself.

Each day you are going to have a magical journey of seeing yourself as the amazing, gorgeous creature that you are!

It may be uncomfortable at first. But, I also know from experience that it will get easier as each day goes by.

There may be some days where focusing on some body parts may be more sensitive than others. If you've experienced the trauma of a hysterectomy or breast removal, you may think "Heather, I don't have these parts, so I don't have anything to be grateful for in regards to that part."

This is where I want to stretch you to think about what you were grateful for when you did have them. How did they serve you at the time? And, now that you don't have them, what good things have you been able to experience in life.

When we look through the lenses of finding what's right and good, we will always find it. This is the muscle I intend for this book to help grow.

After reading the story for each day, here is what you will do to create a smarter, sexier, happier you!

For best results, I recommend that you do the *morning* steps first thing in the morning (you'll be guided through this each day), *during the day* step(s) periodically throughout your day, and the *evening* steps at the end of your day.

it's time to get naked!

morning

• Set a timer for 1 minute. It's important to take the time to take in the whole of your body. (I know for some, 1 minute may seem like an eternity, trust me, it will get easier. If you need to start off with 30 seconds, you can do that and then incrementally work your way up to a minute.)

Look at yourself naked in the mirror. Scan your body from head to toe. Stand in awe at the brilliance that is your body. There is no one else like you on this earth! Thank your body for being the physical manifestation of who you are.

2. As you look at yourself naked in the mirror, state the Positive Vibration Statement (PVS) for that day (daily PVS are explained on the next page).

You'll want to repeat the PVS periodically throughout your day; when you are walking, driving, working out are all great times to say your PVS. The more motion and emotion you say it with, the more it will become who you are.

Whenever you are moving (walking, climbing stairs, working out etc.), say the PVS out loud. If you are in a public place and are concerned that people might think you need to be committed to you local psychiatric ward, just visualize saying it aloud to yourself.

You can also have fun by singing the PVS to the tune of whatever song is on the radio. Depending on the tune, it can be very funny to adapt the words to the song, and you end up laughing along the way. (Rumor has it there is nothing sexier on a woman than a smile).

3. As you look at yourself naked in the mirror, focus your eyes on the body part for the day. Thank it for being a part of you. Imagine what life would be like without it, then express gratitude for how it has helped you.

4. Write down 5 things about that body part that you are or could be grateful for.

If you have a hard time finding something to be grateful for with that specific part, say this to yourself, "I know there is nothing to be grateful for about my _____, but if there were it would be ____ (and fill in the blank)."

5. As you dress for the day express gratitude for the body you have to decorate with different clothes.

during the day

As you go through the day, repeat the PVS periodically. When you are walking, driving, working out are all great times to say your PVS. The more motion and emotion you say it with, the more it will become who you are.

evening

1. At the end of the day, review the 5 things you wrote down in step 4 about that day's body part. As you read each one aloud, say, "Thank you, thank you, thank you" and really allow yourself to feel the gratitude for the amazingness that is your body with each expression.

2. Before you go to bed, say the PVS one more time and thank that body part for being uniquely yours.

What is a Positive Vibration Statement?

In the personal development world there is a high value placed on saying positive statements--some call them affirmations, others call them incantations. These are short, powerful statements that you declare to be true. The idea is that when you say them with conviction and passion while engaging your whole body when saying them, you will re-wire your neural pathways, creating new beliefs.

Personally, I struggled with saying affirmations/ incantations because it felt inauthentic to say a statement such as "I love myself" when I was at a low point in my life.

What I didn't understand at the time is that everything in life is energy. There is positive, negative and neutral energy--each of those energies has a vibration to them ranging from low to high. When we are living in a state of self-hatred or dislike towards ourselves, we are living in a negative energy.

That negative energy has a low vibration to it--we know it and can feel it, yet we often don't know what to do to get beyond it. What is challenging about being in this state is that when we make these statements because we are told it will help, we feel frustrated because we don't believe what we are saying so we don't say them.

What I eventually came to understand is that when we make these statements, we are actually stating words and phrases that are raising our level of vibration. I realized that, even though I didn't necessarily believe it at the time, the worlds that I was saying were working to develop a positive vibration in my body, mind and soul, which is what I desired. Once I looked at it from that perspective, I felt more in alignment with what I was saying.

Before I made this switch, many of my clients, when asked if they did their affirmations or incantations would respond, "I did it once but it felt so in-authentic to me so I stopped."

When I began teaching them about saying Positive Vibration Statements (PVS) that would raise their level of vibration from low to high they found them much easier to say consistently and would experience shifts in their beliefs as they said them each day.

If you've ever struggled with saying incantations or affirmations, I invite you to think about them in this way. Our words create our reality; saying Positive Vibration Statements (PVS) daily will raise your energy and allow you to create the positive beliefs that you desire.

As a woman, I've found that singing my PVS allows me to be more in my femininity. Also, saying them when I give myself a dance break, taking a walk or jumping on my mini-trampoline brings fun to saying them.

When you are saying your PVS, try different things to see what works to create a level of fun for you.

Now, let the 28 days naked begin!

day 1: *luxurious hair*

Loving oneself isn't hard, when you understand who and what 'yourself' is. It has nothing to do with the shape of your face, the size of your eyes, the length of your hair or the quality of your clothes. It's so beyond all of those things and it's what gives life to everything about you. Your own self is such a treasure.

Phylicia Rashad

day 1: *hair*

positive vibration statement

My hair is amazing. I deeply and completely love & accept my glorious hair.

day 1: *hair*

Do you love your hair?

I don't think I'd be alone in saying that I have wished my hair were different. It isn't straight. It isn't curly. Left on it's own, it definitely isn't smooth and silky.

Why couldn't it be like the hair of the models I saw in magazines? Why couldn't I go outside in the summer without looking like a frizz factory?

It wasn't until I had a conversation a few years ago with a friend who suffered from Alopecia (an Auto-immune disease where the immune system mistakenly attacks hair follicles and causes hair loss) that I realized I had all of my own hair, something I had taken for granted up to that point.

Yes, it is frizzy.

Yes, if I were to not color it, it would be gray (I'm not willing to go there yet).

But I have all of my hair.

We live in a day and age where we have hair products to make it curly or straight. Thank God for hair products.

We have the option to cut it short or let it grow.

To have bangs. Or not.

If we want it longer NOW, we can use extensions.

If we want to put pink or blue or purple in our hair, we can.

Even my friend who has Alopecia can use different all natural wigs to change how she looks.

Today, as you look in the mirror, think about all of the different hairstyles you've had. If you grew up in the era of Perms (I'm totally

day 1: *hair*

dating myself right now) think about how grateful you are that that time is behind you and how your hair survived all of those chemicals!

If you grew up in the 80's living like you had stock in Aqua Net, express gratitude for the fact that you are still living and still have all of your hair.

If you have Alopecia, like my friend, express gratitude for the different wigs you can play around with.

Think about how you can communicate how you are feeling through your hair. When I want to feel playful, I like to wear my hair wavy. When I want to feel sleek and put together, I like to wear my hair poker straight. What creative ways can you use your hair to express yourself?

As you eat and drink ask yourself, will eating this create the luxurious hair that I desire?

Throughout the day, look at your hair and think about how the hair on your head has kept you warm when you were cold and how the hair on your body has protected you from environmental influences.

Yes, maybe it's straight and you always wanted curly hair (or vice-versa), but your hair is your hair and you have the ability to change its style whenever you'd like.

Today, as you wash it, dry it, style it, or run your fingers through it, let your hair know how grateful you are for it. If you shave your arms, legs, bikini or any other area, thank the hair you're shaving that it was there to keep you warm if you needed it. Your hair makes up so much of who you are, so let it know how much you love it today!

day 1: *hair*

it's time to get naked!

morning

1. Set a timer for 1 minute.

Look at yourself naked in the mirror. Scan your body from head to toe. Stand in awe at the brilliance that is your body.

2. As you look at yourself naked in the mirror state today's PVS --

My hair is amazing. I deeply and completely love and accept my glorious hair.

3. Focus your eyes on your hair. Thank it for being a part of you.

4. Write down 5 things you are or could be grateful for about your hair (the hair on your head or your body hair).

♥ _____

♥ _____

♥ _____

♥ _____

♥ _____

5. As you do your hair today, express gratitude that you have the ability to change how you look by how you style your hair.

day 1: *hair*

during the day

Repeat today's hair PVS whenever you touch your hair throughout the day.

evening

1. At the end of the day review your 5 reasons to be grateful for your hair. Say, "Thank you, thank you, thank you" to your hair and feel the gratitude for the amazingness that is your body after each expression of gratitude.

2. Before you go to bed, say today's PVS one more time and thank your hair for being uniquely yours.

God gave you gift of 86,400 seconds today. Have you used one to say 'thank you'?

William A Ward

… day 2: *eyes*

day 2: *eyes that shine*

For beautiful eyes, look for the good in others; for beautiful lips, speak only words of kindness; and for poise, walk with the knowledge that you are never alone.

Audrey Hepburn

day 2: *eyes*

positive vibration statement
I love my eyes. I see the world and myself clearly. My eyes give light to the world.

day 2: *eyes*

They say that our eyes are the windows to our souls. When you look into someone's eyes you can easily tell if they are sad, happy, tired, or elated. Without ever hearing someone speak, we can gather a lot of information about someone just by looking into his or her eyes.

We can tell if someone is healthy by the brightness of the whites of their eyes, we can tell if someone is hiding something by their refusal to allow you to look into their eyes, and eyes that shine are incredibly inviting.

Just as our fingerprints have their own unique characteristics, the different structure of lines, dots, and colors in our eyes creates our own unique iris. No one in the world has the same eyes as you do.

With the ability to distinguish about 10 million colors, your eye is the fastest muscle in your body and is compromised of over 200 million working parts. After the brain, the eyes are the most complex organs we have.

Meant to keep the dirt out of our eyes and act as a first defense against bugs, dust, and other irritants, eyelashes have an average lifespan of five months.

Ever wonder why people have eyebrows? They are there to prevent sweat from dripping into one's eyes (salty sweat in the eye is the worst).

Our eyes are absolutely amazing. Imagine what your life would be like if you didn't have the ability to see all of the colors you are seeing right now. Think about all of the memories you wouldn't have if you didn't have your sight.

Imagine if you didn't have the ability to navigate through life so easily because you didn't have your sight.

In my early 20's I worked as an optometric technician (I was the person that gave all of the pre-tests you receive before seeing the doctor, including the dreaded "puff" test for glaucoma).

day 2: *eyes*

I was so excited to get the job because I would have access to colored contact lenses (I always wanted to have brown eyes). I remember thinking about how I would finally have the ability to change how I looked—at least how my eyes looked.

When I wasn't able to master the art of contact lenses I had to concede that God (nature, whatever you believe in) intentionally gave me blue eyes and that maybe I should be grateful that they worked.

What are you grateful for when it comes to your eyes? When someone looks at you do they see someone who is happy, healthy, excited, and in love with life, or do they see someone who is sad, lifeless, and full of illness?

Spend 1 minute looking into your eyes and thanking your higher power for the gift of your eyes.

As you go throughout your day, whenever you see something or someone you don't like, express gratitude that you have the ability to look away, and that you have seen enough beauty to know what isn't beautiful.

Imagine as if you were seeing everything for the first time today; look at each item with wonder and revel in it.

It may sound Polly-Anna but you'll be surprised how your day will turn out when you do it!

day 2: *eyes*

it's time to get naked!

morning

1. Set a timer for 1 minute.

Look at yourself naked in the mirror, scanning your body from head to toe, standing in awe at the brilliance that is your body.

2. As you look at yourself naked in the mirror state today's PVS --

I love my eyes. I see the world and myself clearly. My eyes give light to the world.

3. Focus your attention on your eyes. As awkward as it may feel, stare deeply into your eyes, and thank them for all they do for you.

4. Write down 5 things you are or could be grateful for about your eyes.

♥ _____

♥ _____

♥ _____

♥ _____

♥ _____

5. If you wear make-up, express gratitude for the ability to play around with different kinds of make-up to highlight your eyes.

day 2: *eyes*

during the day

Each time you see a piece of beauty today or look in the mirror, wink at beauty or yourself and be grateful for your eyes.

evening

1. At the end of the day review your 5 reasons to be grateful for your eyes. Say, "Thank you, thank you, thank you" to your eyes and feel the gratitude for the amazingness that is your eyes.

2. Before you go to bed, say the PVS one more time and thank your eyes for being uniquely yours.

> *As we express our gratitude, we must never forget that the highest appreciation is not to utter words, but to live by them.*
>
> John F. Kennedy

day 3: *ears to hear*

We have two ears and one tongue so that we would listen more and talk less.

Diogenes

day 3: *ears*

positive vibration statement
My ears are amazing. I listen with both ears to hear the delight and joy that surrounds me.

day 3: *ears*

What's your favorite song?

Can't pick one and now you have a few different songs changing in your head? That's what happens to me.

What's your favorite nature sound?

The wind rustling through the trees? The sound of rain on a rooftop? A waterfall? A babbling brook? The sound of children laughing? The ocean lapping the shores?

There are so many great sounds, it's hard to pick just one.

Granted. I'm going to say this about every part of our bodies, but our ears ARE absolutely amazing.

Did you know that the three bones that make up the ear, stapes (stirrup), malleus (hammer) and incus (anvil) are so small that they can be placed together on a penny?

It's amazing that something so tiny impacts our world in such big ways.

The visible part of our ear, the outer ear, or Pinna, directs sound further inside the ear through the external auditory canal, which leads to the eardrum in the middle ear (Tympanic cavity).

The middle ear or Tympanic cavity is where those three tiny bones are found. After sound passes through the outer ear, it comes to the middle ear, and makes the eardrum vibrate. The vibrations are picked up by those three tiny bones and amplify the sound.

Then the inner ear, which houses a network of passages and tubes referred to as labyrinth, transforms the sounds into electrical impulses through the help of the small snail shell-like organ known as cochlea.

Those impulses are then sent to the brain's auditory center using auditory nerves and, just like that, we can hear! Remarkable, right?

day 3: *ears*

Not only do our ears allow us to hear, they also keep equilibrium balanced between body pressure and the atmospheric pressure. If you've ever been high up on a mountain you may have experienced dizziness, discomfort, and ear pain. That's because the Eustachian tube fails to maintain pressure. Apparently we aren't exactly equipped to be high up in the mountains!

Imagine what your life would be like without your ability to hear. It sounds silly but imagine how quiet life would be.

As you go throughout your day, every time you hear a noise that hurts your ears, express thanks that you have the ears to hear.

When you hear a sound you love, whether it's your favorite song or the voice of someone you love, express gratitude for that beautiful sound.

At the end of the day, think through your day remembering all of the glorious sounds you have heard. Let the world know how grateful you are to have heard its entire symphony of sounds!

day 3: *ears*

it's time to get naked!

morning

1. Set a timer for 1 minute.

Look at yourself naked in the mirror, scanning your body from head to toe, standing in awe at the brilliance that is your body.

2. As you look at yourself naked in the mirror state today's PVS –

My ears are amazing. I listen with both ears to hear the delight and joy that surrounds me.

3. Focus your attention on your ears. Notice how they are shaped, and how when you are silent, they hear more than you consciously notice throughout the day.

4. Write down 5 things you are or could be grateful for about your ears.

♥
_____

♥
_____

♥
_____

♥
_____

♥
_____

5. If you wear earrings, choose a beautiful pair today and express gratitude for the ability to decorate your ears differently each day.

day 3: *ears*

during the day

Whenever you hear something unusual today or touch your ears or earrings, say a silent 'thank you' to your ears.

evening

1. At the end of the day review your 5 reasons to be grateful for your ears. Say, "Thank you, thank you, thank you" to your ears and feel the gratitude for the amazingness of your ears.

2. Before you go to bed, say the PVS one more time and thank your ears for being uniquely yours.

Happiness cannot be traveled to, owned, earned, worn or consumed. Happiness is the spiritual experience of living every minute with love, grace, and gratitude.

Denis Waitley

day 4: *smiling mouth*

My smile is my favorite part of my body. I think a smile can make your whole body.

Serena Williams

day 4: *mouth*

positive vibration statement

I love my mouth. I feed my body healthy nourishing food. I speak words of life and love to myself everyday.

day 4: *mouth*

My whole life my mouth has been a focal point of insecurity for me.

When I was in elementary school I fell over the handlebars of my bike and busted my top lip. Years later, as my upper gum was turning black, we realized I had killed my front right tooth (it pains me to even write about it now.)

In 7th grade I had a root canal that was supposed to make things better—it didn't. My gum increasingly grew darker and darker.

Then, my freshman year of high school I chipped the front left tooth. In my mind I felt like I looked like someone who had been living homeless in the Appalachian Mountains with no dental care.

On top of that, I hated that I had such small lips. I thought that if God was going to give me crappy teeth, the least he could have done was give me big, full lips.

A bit dramatic? Absolutely! Don't we all have those moments?

By the time I was in my early 20s the dead nerves in my gum that was turning it black were too much for me to bear. I hated the way I looked and did not feel confident smiling so I had my tooth replaced with a crown.

I remember sitting in the dentist chair as if it were yesterday. She drilled down the dead tooth until it was just a little nub then left the room to get the crown. As she was leaving she said, "Don't look in the mirror while I'm gone."

"Really? You say that to me right before you leave the room knowing there's a hand mirror right next to me?" I thought.
So, I did what any of us would do. I picked up the mirror and smiled. Absolutely horrified, I had to stop myself from screaming.

My biggest fears had come true. My left front tooth was just a little nub of blackness, and the tooth next to it was chipped. I believed I actually looked as if I was that person who had been living homeless in the Appalachian Mountains never having any dental care.

day 4: *mouth*

As tears streamed down my face, the dentist walked back in and scolded me for having done what she told me not to do, which did not make me feel better.

After she put in the crown and bonded the chipped tooth, the person I saw in the mirror was completely different. I had a beautiful smile. All of my teeth were white and straight. My confidence began to grow with each smile.

Until about 10 years later, that crown decided that it wanted to start dropping and became uneven with the tooth next to it.

Sigh... I felt like I was back to where I started, looking like a homeless mountain lady, not proud of my smile.

My theme song was *All I Want For Christmas Is My Two Front Teeth*. No lie.

Determined to not have horrible teeth for the rest of my life I found another dentist who convinced me that the bonded chipped tooth would be more aesthetically appealing if it was a crown as well. He also said he could re-do the original crown and he promised to use higher quality material for lasting results.

So, there I was again, having my tooth drilled down to a little nub. Thankfully no one left me alone in the room with a mirror this time so I wasn't tempted to look in the mirror.

After he finished his work, and I finally checked the mirror, I was absolutely amazed. I had the smile that I had always wanted. Not one person could tell that both front teeth were crowns. I was so proud of my smile that I smiled so much for the next few months that my cheeks hurt.

What was interesting about this whole process was that I realized that to me, having nice teeth was so much of my identity. I thought that if people saw me for who I *really* was, someone with horrendous teeth, they would see that I was actually—ugly.

day 4: *mouth*

I had given so much meaning to having great teeth and had forgotten that the sum of who I am is not my teeth or my lips. My beauty doesn't come from any single part of my body.

Certainly, our bodies are a reflection of who we are. What we eat, what we think, how we move, and what we drink create either health or disease. So we do have control over much of how we look.

I was confusing that with the story I had created--that because I had a busted tooth from a childhood bike accident, I was ugly. It's crazy the stories we make up, isn't it?

What was truly ugly was the story that I believed about myself. Once I decided to give up that story and started believing that I was beautiful, my smile made more of an appearance and my confidence increased.

The reality is, our mouths are absolutely amazing, even with a couple of bum teeth. Our lips, teeth, gums and tongue work for us every second to experience life in amazing ways.

The mouth itself is the first stage of digestion as our teeth and our saliva begin the process of breaking down food.

Our tongues, soft palate, and cheek epiglottis house our taste buds (the majority of them being on our tongues), which give us a sense of taste. Imagine how boring eating would be if we didn't have the pleasure of tasting sweet, salty, bitter, sour, and umami.

We communicate with our words through our mouth. Imagine what your life would be like if you were unable to speak.

When I lived in the space of hating my teeth and my lips I missed out on so much goodness life has to offer. Instead of being present in each moment and enjoying the people I was with, I often found myself focusing on myself and how terrible my teeth looked.

As I began to express gratitude for my teeth, lips, tongue, and all parts of my mouth, life became much richer.

day 4: *mouth*

If you don't like your teeth, express gratitude that we have dental professionals that can help with our challenges.

Think about all of the foods your teeth have processed over the course of your life and express gratitude for that.

Think about the people you have kissed with your lips. Smile and express gratitude for them.

Think about how your tongue has allowed you to taste so many different flavors.

As you go throughout your day, each time you bite into food, open your mouth to speak, look in the mirror to put on lipstick, express gratitude for your mouth and everything it's done for you, and see if life tastes sweeter.

Then smile…because, as Serena Williams said, "a smile can make a whole body."

day 4: *mouth*

it's time to get naked!

morning

1. Set a timer for 1 minute.

Look at yourself naked in the mirror, scanning your body from head to toe, standing in awe of the brilliance that is your body.

2. As you look at yourself naked in the mirror state today's PVS –

I love my mouth. I feed my body healthy nourishing food. I speak words of life and love to myself everyday.

3. Focus your attention on your mouth. Notice the shape of your lips and your tongue as well as the size of your teeth.

4. Write down 5 things you are or could be grateful for about your mouth.

♥ _____

♥ _____

♥ _____

♥ _____

♥ _____

day 4: *mouth*

during the day

As you brush your teeth, floss, or touch up your lipstick or lip-gloss, express gratitude for every part that makes up your mouth.

evening

1. At the end of the day review your 5 reasons to be grateful for your mouth. Say, "Thank you, thank you, thank you" to your mouth and feel the gratitude for the amazingness that is your mouth.

2. Before you go to bed, say the PVS one more time and thank your mouth for being uniquely yours.

Develop an attitude of gratitude, and give thanks for everything that happens to you, knowing that every step forward is a step toward achieving something bigger and better than your current situation.

Brian Tracy

day 5: *precious nose*

For young women, I would say, don't worry so much about your weight. Girls spend way too much time thinking about that, and there are better things. For young men, and women, too, what makes you different or weird, that's your strength ... I used to hate my nose. Now I don't. It's OK.

Meryl Steep

day 5: *nose*

positive vibration statement
I love my nose. I am grateful for the breath it takes in that creates my being and the smells it allows me to experience.

day 5: *nose*

From the time he could speak my younger brother would tease me about the bump I have on the bridge of my nose. He'd take his finger and act as if he were skiing down my nose using the bump to project his finger into the air.

I can't help but laugh when I think about it now, but growing up I was so insecure about my nose. Avoiding profile pictures was an art form.

In my 20s I had seriously contemplated getting a nose job. Fortunately, I didn't have the extra cash for it, so I was forced to learn to love the nose I was given.

Whether you love or hate the shape of your nose, you can't help but be impressed with its abilities.

It generally takes having a cold to remind us how much it impacts our quality of life, our energy levels, and our ability to breathe and sleep.

Our noses filter and humidify the air we breathe before it enters our lungs, so that we don't get dust and germs in our lungs.

Did you know that each day your nose and sinuses produce about one quart of mucus, which contains infection-fighting enzymes and white blood cells, and helps humidify the inhaled air and wash the nasal walls of filtered particles?

A quart seems like a lot of mucus to expel doesn't it? We actually swallow much of it and if the air we inhale is dry it will absorb water from the mucus, leaving it flaky or pasty—otherwise known as snot or boogies.

Our noses also give us the ability to detect more than 10,000 scents because of the olfactory sensors on the ceiling of the nasal cavity. Those sensors activate finger-like receptors that transmit chemical signals to the olfactory bulb in your brain, which registers scent.

What's even more fascinating is that our sense of smell is the only one of the five senses that has a direct pathway to our brains hippocampus,

day 5: *nose*

which is involved in memory formation, and the amygdala, which processes emotion and memory.

What that means is that smells create emotions for us faster than any other sense. It is way more powerful than we often give it credit.

What would life be like to not smell onions sautéing, fresh cut flowers, the ocean air, or cinnamon buns baking in the oven?

Whatever your relationship has been like with your nose, today, make it one of gratitude. It was given to you exactly as it is to give you your own unique experience with the world. Let it know how grateful you are for it and the precious things it does for you.

day 5: *nose*

it's time to get naked!

morning

1. Set a timer for 1 minute.

Look at yourself naked in the mirror, scanning your body from head to toe, standing in awe of the brilliance that is your body.

2. As you look at yourself naked in the mirror state today's PVS --

I love my nose. I am grateful for the breath it takes in that creates my being and the smells it allows me to experience.

3. Focus your attention on your nose. Notice its shape and size. Feel the air that is keeping you alive as you inhale and exhale.

4. Write down 5 things you are or could be grateful for about your nose.

♥ _____

♥ _____

♥ _____

♥ _____

♥ _____

day 5: *nose*

during the day

Each time you smell something today, take a deep breath and be grateful for your nose.

evening

1. At the end of the day review your 5 reasons to be grateful for your mouth. Say, "Thank you, thank you, thank you" to your nose and feel the gratitude for the amazingness that is your nose.

2. Before you go to bed, say the PVS one more time and thank your nose for being uniquely yours.

The antidote to fear is gratitude. The antidote to anger is gratitude. You can't feel fear or anger while feeling gratitude at the same time.

Tony Robbins

day 6: *cheekbones created from a genuine smile*

Everyone has something that is their asset, some have the hair, some have the cheekbones, other have the lips. But once you know what your asset is, then you should capitalize on it.

Blue Cantrell

day 6: *cheeks*

positive vibration statement
I love my cheekbones. It's okay for me to like myself, its okay to love myself.

day 6: *cheeks*

If I'm completely honest, before coming up with a list of body parts to focus on for this book, cheekbones were not something I focused on.

Don't get me wrong, I focused on them enough to know the appropriate spot to place blush, but other than that I never thought much about them.

Western culture tells us that a woman who has high cheekbones is considered attractive.

It's thought that this Western obsession with cheekbones started with Katherine Hepburn whose beauty graced the silver screen. While I can't argue that women like Katherine Hepburn, Kate Moss, and Naomi Campbell are very attractive, I believe that there is so much more that makes a woman attractive than her cheekbones.

The shine that comes through your eyes when you smile, the glow of your skin when you are eating a clean diet, the confidence that exudes from you when you love yourself unconditionally are all qualities that outweigh any bronzer, highlighter, or filler used to create chiseled cheekbones. Makeup washes off; unconditional love for oneself cannot be washed off. A genuine smile creates gorgeous cheekbones faster than any make up artist ever could.

Today, as you look at yourself naked, really look at your face. Check out your cheekbones. Think about how they make up exactly who you are. Even if you have an identical twin or you've found your doppelganger, your face is exactly how it is meant to be—they may look like you but there are not exactly you.

Smile the biggest smile you can. Notice how your cheekbones create your unique face. Yes, you can highlight, contour, and bronze to accentuate and have some fun with makeup but at the end of the day, your cheekbones are exactly how they are supposed to be. Thank them for where they are placed. Thank them for how they make your face uniquely yours.

day 6: *cheeks*

it's time to get naked!

morning

1. Set a timer for 1 minute.

Look at yourself naked in the mirror, scanning your body from head to toe, standing in awe of the brilliance that is your body.

2. As you look at yourself naked in the mirror state today's PVS --

I love my cheekbones. It's okay for me to like myself; it's okay to love myself.

3. Focus your attention on your cheekbones. As you smile, notice their shape and how they define much of your face.

4. Write down 5 things you are or could be grateful for about your cheekbones.

♥
_____

♥
_____

♥
_____

♥
_____

♥
_____

5. If you use make up, notice how the blush you choose can completely transform how your cheekbones appear.

day 6: *cheeks*

during the day

Each time you look in the mirror today, notice your cheekbones and smile.

Evening

1. At the end of the day review your 5 reasons to be grateful for your cheekbones. Say, "Thank you, thank you, thank you" to your cheekbones and feel the gratitude for the amazingness that is your cheekbones.

2. Before you go to bed, say the PVS one more time and thank your cheekbones for being uniquely yours.

'Thank you' is the best prayer that anyone could say. I say that one a lot. Thank you expresses extreme gratitude, humility, understanding.

Alice Walker

day 6: *cheeks*

day 7: *keep your chin up*

So keep your head high, keep your chin up, and most importantly, keep smiling, because life's a beautiful thing and there's so much to smile about.

Marilyn Monroe

day 7: *chin*

positive vibration statement
I love my chin. Everyday and every way my mind and body gets smarter and sexier.

day 7: *chin*

Every summer my parents took my siblings and me camping. One summer in particular, when I was around 11 or 12, we visited a county fair where there was an artist doing caricature drawings.

Caricature drawings are intentional distortions of the subject, over-maximizing the distinctive features or peculiarities of the subject. We've all seen pictures of Jay Leno with his chin over-emphasized or Mick Jagger's lips enlarged. When we see them we chuckle because we know there is some element of truth to the picture.

My parents decided that it would be a good idea to have this guy create a caricature of the three of us children AND it would be a profile caricature.

In day 5, I told you about my insecurities about my nose and always avoiding profile pictures. After this caricature drawing was complete I had something else to be insecure about. I never knew my chin was so pronounced. My brother loved pointing that out, and from that day forward I literally felt as if my chin stuck out farther than my face.

Like my desire to get a nose job, I seriously considered having my chin worked on as well. I thought that if the doctors could just shave off a little bit of it, I wouldn't look so bad and I'd be happy.

What I realized as I grew up was that so many of the "pretty" girls I knew weren't happy either. They had the same feelings I did. There were things about their bodies they wanted to change that I would have loved to have.

I realized that my happiness was never going to come from how I looked. A new outfit, haircut, or makeup job may make me momentarily happy, but it would not bring lasting happiness.

My happiness had to come from the inside. Being in a place of gratitude, appreciating everything that has been given to me, being present with myself, my feelings, and other people as well as deepening my relationship with my creator all create a happiness that cannot be taken away.

day 7: *chin*

The moment we focus on all the things we don't have, on external things, events, and outcomes, we lose a little bit of ourselves.

Happiness is something we choose or don't choose every moment. When we live in a place of gratitude for who we are and the abundance that has been given to us, life is magical.

The shape of my chin has little bearing on my happiness--unless I choose to give it the meaning that it has to be perfect in order for me to be happy. If I do that, then I will constantly be chasing happiness. And really, how exhausting is that?

When I learned to embrace all of the other perceived "flaws" I saw on my face, keep my chin up, and step into a place of gratitude for the fact that God created my face exactly how he wanted it to be, my life became so much more fun, free, and happy.

Today, every time you look at yourself in the mirror, express gratitude for your chin. It is exactly the way it was meant to be and without it, you wouldn't look like you!

day 7: *chin*

it's time to get naked!

morning

1. Set a timer for 1 minute.

Look at yourself naked in the mirror, scanning your body from head to toe, standing in awe of the brilliance that is your body.

2. As you look at yourself naked in the mirror state today's PVS --

I love my chin.
Everyday and every way my mind and body gets smarter and sexier.

3. Focus your attention on your chin. Check it out from the front and the side views, and thank it for being your chin.

4. Write down 5 things you are or could be grateful for about your chin.

♥ _____

♥ _____

♥ _____

♥ _____

♥ _____

day 7: *chin*

during the day

Take a moment to notice your chin each time you look in the mirror today. Lift it up and smile in gratitude for all it takes each day.

evening

1. At the end of the day review your 5 reasons to be grateful for your chin. Say, "Thank you, thank you, thank you" to your chin and feel the gratitude for the amazingness that is your chin.

2. Before you go to bed, say the PVS one more time and thank your chin for being uniquely yours.

Gratitude makes sense of our past, brings peace for today, and creates a vision for tomorrow.

Melody Beattle

day 8: *stick your neck out*

Behold the turtle. He only makes progress when he sticks his neck out.

James Bryant Conant

day 8: *neck*

positive vibration statement
I love my neck. I am thankful for my neck that moves with ease.

day 8: *neck*

Did you see the 2002 movie, *My Big Fat Greek Wedding*? One of my favorite scenes is when the mother (Maria) and daughter (Toula) are having a conversation about how stubborn Toula thinks her dad is. Her mom replies to her complaint:

"The man is the head, but the woman is the neck. And she can turn the head any way she wants."

What is great about that line is that it gives attention to a part of our body that doesn't often get as much attention as it deserves—our necks. (And, it sheds a lot of truth on who really does run things. They say behind every good man is a good woman…)

Our amazing neck houses seven of the smallest vertebrae and approximately 29 muscles connecting our spine and torso to our heads.

Here's an interesting fact: the human neck has the same number of vertebrae as a giraffe's neck. No one really knows why our necks aren't as long as a giraffe's neck, but no matter what the reason, I'm definitely grateful that my neck isn't that long.

Our neck also houses our larynx, which houses our vocal cords, which give us the ability to speak.

When I was on a mission trip in high school my best friend and I decided that we didn't like the sound of our voices so we decided to go "on strike" and stopped talking. That lasted for about an hour until we decided that it was too quite and we didn't know how to communicate our needs so we started talking again.

As silly as that little strike was, it made me very aware of how important my voice is in communication.

It is said that only 7% of any message is conveyed through spoken words, yet the ability to speak is such a great gift.

The larynx divides into two parts: the trachea, the tube that carries air to the lungs, and the esophagus, the tube that carries food to the stomach.

day 8: *neck*

I don't know about you, but I often forget about how many functions need to happen to do two things I adore doing--breathing and eating. So much of that happens in our necks.

Our neck also houses our thyroid gland, which produces hormones that regulate our bodies' metabolic rate as well as heart and digestive function, muscle control, brain development, and bone maintenance. Without our thyroid functioning properly we can experience symptoms such as fatigue, weight gain or loss, mood swings, dry skin, and trouble sleeping, just to name a few.

In addition to giving us goose bumps when our lover gently kisses it, the neck serves as such an important part for overall health.

When the vertebrae in our necks are functioning properly we have the ability to look all around us—we can look down at the beautiful grass on the ground, up to the fluffy clouds, and to our sides to see those we love.

When was the last time you looked at your neck? I mean really looked at your neck and expressed gratitude for everything it does for you each day?

Today, stick your neck out for your own well-being and say "thank You" for all that it does for you that goes unnoticed. Let it know how much you appreciate it.

day 8: *neck*

it's time to get naked!

morning

1. Set a timer for 1 minute.

Look at yourself naked in the mirror, scanning your body from head to toe, standing in awe of the brilliance that is your body.

2. As you look at yourself naked in the mirror state today's PVS --

I love my neck. I am thankful for my neck that moves with ease.

3. Focus your attention on your neck. As you look at it, imagine all of the functions–breathing, eating, and speaking—that go on beneath the surface of your skin working to make you, you.

4. If you like to wear necklaces, pick one today that highlights your exquisite neck.

5. Write down 5 things you are or could be grateful for about your neck.

♥ _____

♥ _____

♥ _____

♥ _____

♥ _____

day 8: *neck*

during the day

Whenever you touch your necklace or your neck today or eat, thank your neck and your throat for all it does for you.

evening

1. At the end of the day review your 5 reasons to be grateful for your neck. Say, "Thank you, thank you, thank you" to your neck and feel the gratitude for the amazingness that is your neck.

2. Before you go to bed, say the PVS one more time and thank your neck for being uniquely yours.

When I started counting my blessings, my whole life turned around.

Willie Nelson

day 9: *i got your back*

You only really discover the strength of your spine when your back is against the wall.

James Geary

day 9: *back*

positive vibration statement

I love my back. I love how it supports me every day and carries me through life with ease.

day 9: *back*

Unless you recently had a tattoo put on your back, chances are you don't make a conscious effort to look at your back on a daily basis.

Yet, you may be one of the approximately 31 million Americans who have experienced low-back pain at any given time. According to the Global Burden of Disease 2010, low back pain is the single leading cause of disability worldwide.

Experts estimate that as many as 80% of the population will experience a back problem at some time in their lives and they say that the most common cause of back pain and spinal chord trauma in America is car accidents.

The spine is the main pathway of communication between the brain and the rest of the body. When our spine is out of alignment we can experience muscle spasms, dizziness, low energy, headaches, poor digestion, and general pain.

As one who has experienced the "joys" of back pain, due to a car accident from 20 years ago, I can honestly say when the back is in pain, it's no joke. It impacts one's mental, emotional, spiritual, and physical worlds, sometimes in ways we cannot even comprehend.

When the spine is operating correctly and is supporting the body's weight, providing flexibility for movement and protecting nerve roots and fibers, life is amazing.

In 1994, I was a passenger in a car accident that caused severe back pain until 2013. After the accident, I was taken to the hospital, and I clearly remember standing for the x-ray, feeling like I had a thousand pound weight on my right shoulder. The x-rays did not show any breaks, so the doctors sent me home.

I knew something was terribly wrong, but being young I felt like my voice wouldn't be heard if I said anything, so I said nothing. There is nothing worse than being told that 'nothing is wrong with you' when you know at the core of your being that something is terribly wrong.

day 9: *back*

I felt like Humpty-Dumpty. I was broken but there was no one there to put me back together again.

For the next 18 years I had knots in my shoulder blades that I swore had their own zip code and every time someone gave me a massage they asked what was wrong with my neck because my vertebrae seemed to be larger than normal. The level of pain I was in on a scale of 1-10 was constantly was a 20.

It wasn't until 2013 when I started seeing a Rolfer. Rolfing is an amazing form of bodywork with a terrible name. Rolfing is aimed at providing realignment of the entire body through deliberate, accurate, and targeted movement of the fascia, the thin sheath of fibrous tissue enclosing a muscle or organ.

After 10 weekly sessions of Rolfing, I went from level 20 pain to a level .05. Life literally changed for me. My moods were better, my energy levels increased, and I could do things pain-free that I had not done without pain for the past 20 years.

I was finally put back together again! An experience like that can make you really grateful for a back that works correctly.

If you have experienced back pain, you know what I am referring to. If you've never experienced back pain, you are very fortunate.
Either way, I invite you to pay extra-special attention to your back today. Each time it touches the back of a chair say, "Thank you, back, for all of your support." Each time you bend over to pick up something say, "Thank you, back, for being so flexible"

Each time you twist at the waist to look at something behind you say, "Thank you, back, for your strength."

As you walk throughout the day, instead of waiting for someone else to say, "I got your back," "get" your own back by repeating the day's PVS: *I love my back. I love how it supports me every day and carries me through life with ease.*

Be in awe at how supportive your back really is for you.

day 9: *back*

it's time to get naked!

morning

1. Set a timer for 1 minute.

Look at yourself naked in the mirror, scanning your body from head to toe, standing in awe of the brilliance that is your body.

2. As you look at yourself naked in the mirror state today's PVS –

I love my back. I love how it supports me every day and carries me through life with ease.

3. Focus your attention on your back (you may need to turn around to look at it). Look at how it holds you upright and supports you all day long.

4. Write down 5 things you are or could be grateful for about your back.

♥ _____

♥ _____

♥ _____

♥ _____

♥ _____

day 9: *back*

during the day

Periodically today, touch your back and thank it for all the effort it does to keep you upright each day.

evening

1. At the end of the day review your 5 reasons to be grateful for your back. Say, "Thank you, thank you, thank you" to your back and feel the gratitude for the amazingness that is your back.

2. Before you go to bed, say the PVS one more time and thank your back for its amazing support.

Gratitude is the healthiest of all human emotions. The more you express gratitude for what you have, the more likely you will have even more to express gratitude for.

Zig Ziglar

day 10: *breasts, your natural jewels*

> *I think the quality of sexiness comes from within. It is something that is in you or it isn't and it really doesn't have much to do with breasts or thighs or the pout of your lips.*
>
> Sophia Loren

day 10: *breasts*

positive vibration statement
I love my breasts. My breasts are healthy and full.

day 10: *breasts*

Breasts, boobs, jugs, knockers, bosoms, rack, boulders, the "girls," melons ... and my least favorite, tits. Whatever you want to call them, our breasts are part of what sets us apart from men.

When we really think about it, no matter what the size, our breasts are quite magical.

They give life to our children. Without the milk that our breasts develop when we are pregnant, we wouldn't be able to create healthy babies to help them grow into toddlers.

Humorist Dave Barry said, "Scientist now believe the primary biological function of breasts is to make males stupid." I agree with him. Any woman with large breasts knows that if she walks by a man with her breasts even slightly exposed, he stops what he is doing and stares.

If used correctly, your breasts can open doors, pull things down from high shelves, carry heavy items from the store to your car, or whatever else you may need help with—men are very helpful when breasts are involved.

Seriously, I was well into my 20s when I discovered that if I wore a tight shirt and put on a smile I could pretty much get any kind of help I needed from a guy. It's not a super-power I use all the time, but it always comes in handy at just the right time.

If they are large enough, breasts can prop up bowls of coconut milk ice cream when you are in a down mood and want nothing more than to veg out in front of the TV.

If they are just the right size, they can make or break an outfit. They really do have magical powers. They are what make us feminine and make men "stupid."

Sadly, I hear so many women demean the size of their breasts or wish them away because they "get in the way." I'll admit that I've been guilty of this one as it's much harder participating in certain sports and buying cute bikinis when you are well-endowed. It's been a conscious

day 10: *breasts*

effort to remember to be grateful for them when they seem to hinder what I want to accomplish.

What if you were to express appreciation all day for the breasts you've been given? If you didn't have them, you would be a radically different person.

What if you looked at your breasts as culture critic Anne Hollander describes--as a woman's *natural jewels*?

Today, as you look at yourself naked in the mirror, let your girls know how grateful you are that they are yours. They will be grateful you did!

day 10: *breasts*

it's time to get naked!

morning

1. Set a timer for 1 minute.

Look at yourself naked in the mirror, scanning your body from head to toe, standing in awe of the brilliance that is your body.

2. As you look at yourself naked in the mirror state today's PVS --

I love my breasts. My breasts are healthy and full.

3. Focus your attention on your breasts. As you smile, notice their shape and size.

4. If you wear bras, as you choose one for the day, notice how each bra can change the shape of your breasts, which changes how your body looks as a whole. Choose a bra that makes you feel beautiful and sexy.

5. Write down 5 things you are or could be grateful for about your breasts.

♥ _____

♥ _____

♥ _____

♥ _____

♥ _____

day 10: *breasts*

during the day

Whenever you see your chest in a reflection today, lift your breasts a little higher and smile.

evening

1. At the end of the day review your 5 reasons to be grateful for your breasts. Say, "Thank you, thank you, thank you" to your breasts and feel the gratitude for the amazingness of your breasts.

2. Before you go to bed, say the PVS one more time and thank your breasts for being uniquely yours.

I don't have to chase extraordinary moments to find happiness—it's right in front of me if I'm paying attention and practicing gratitude.

Brene´ Brown

day 11: *receive with open arms*

Often people ask how I manage to be happy despite having no arms and no legs. The quick answer is that I have a choice. I can be angry about not having limbs, or I can be thankful that I have a purpose. I chose gratitude.

Nick Vujicic

day 11: *arms*

positive vibration statement

I love my arms. I receive love and abundance with open arms.

day 11: *arms*

The first time I saw a video of Nick Vujicic I was literally blown away.

When you Google him and watch his videos you will see a man who has a heart bigger than the planet and enough passion to impact the world and fill ten football stadiums.

You will also see that Nick was born without arms OR legs, yet seems to be living larger than 98% of the world. Nick's mission, *Life Without Limbs*, is about sharing with others how much God adores them. As you listen to Nick's message, even if you have no belief in a God who adores you, you can't help but be moved and wonder, "If he has no limbs and can live a life full of joy and happiness, maybe I can too."

As you can imagine, life for Nick was not easy growing up. He experienced the same challenges of school, friends, and adolescence as most of us do, yet he also struggled with depression and loneliness.

While most of us go through a period of feeling "different" from everyone else, Nick literally was different than everyone else. As anyone would do, Nick questioned why he was different, the purpose of life, and if he even had a purpose.

For Nick, his answer of whether or not he had a purpose came through his faith in God and Jesus. He credits passion and strength to live a life without limbs to his faith in God and his life has inspired millions.

In addition to traveling around the world sharing God's love with others, Nick is an author, musician, actor, husband, and father. I've seen videos of Nick swimming, diving off high dives, playing golf and soccer—all without arms or legs! In one of his YouTube videos, Nick says,

> "You keep on concentrating on the things you don't have and you sort of forget what you do have. What I've seen in life is a couple of key principles and the first thing is to be thankful...It's a lie to think you are not good enough. It's a lie to think that you aren't worth anything."

day 11: *arms*

Amazing words from a man most people would not blame for choosing to be miserable for not having limbs, yet he chooses to gratitude.

As you go throughout your day, instead of being up in arms about the flab you may have on your arms, I invite you to focus on all of the amazing things your arms do for you--from allowing your hands to shave your legs, to giving hugs, to putting on clothes. There are a million things you can easily do because of your arms. Just in the first hour of the day your arms do more for you than you probably notice. Let's celebrate them today.

With each item you pick up, with each bend of your elbow look at your arms in amazement for everything they do for you, then express gratitude to whomever is your higher power. Allow your body to receive the love and gratitude you give to it with open arms.

And, before you climb into bed tonight, wrap your arms around yourself and give yourself a big hug, because you are valuable, worthy, and adored.

day 11: *arms*

it's time to get naked!

morning

1. Set a timer for 1 minute.

Look at yourself naked in the mirror, scanning your body from head to toe, standing in awe of the brilliance that is your body.

2. As you look at yourself naked in the mirror state today's PVS --

I love my arms. I receive love and abundance with open arms.

3. Focus your attention on your arms. Look at them at different angles--lift them up as if you are reaching to the sky, place them on your hips like Wonder Woman, or just let them hang down your side. Thank them for all of the work they do for you throughout the day.

4. Write down 5 things you are or could be grateful for about your arms.

♥ _____

♥ _____

♥ _____

♥ _____

♥ _____

day 11: *arms*

during the day

As you reach for items today, thank your arms for their ability to move and stretch.

evening

1. At the end of the day review your 5 reasons to be grateful for your arms. Say, "Thank you, thank you, thank you" to your arms and feel the gratitude for the amazingness that is your arms.

2. Before you go to bed, say the PVS one more time and thank your arms for being uniquely yours.

Better to lose count while naming your blessings than to lose your blessings to counting your troubles.

Maltbie D. Babcock

day 12: *hands on*

Letting go helps us to live in a more peaceful state of mind and helps restore our balance. It allows others to be responsible for themselves and for us to take our hands off situations that do not belong to us. This frees us from unnecessary stress.

Melody Beattie

day 12: *hands*

positive vibration statement

I love my hands. I choose to receive all things wonderful with open hands.

day 12: *hands*

If you were to meet me in real life and we became close friends you would eventually find out that I have some strange things going on with my hands.

On my right hand my pointer finger has an extra crease in between the upper and middle joints. The crease looks as if there is a joint there but there isn't one. From Googling it I found out that it's called "Extra Inter-Phalangeal Crease." Sounds so official, eh?

Unfortunately, my Google search didn't give me a reason why I have this nor have I met anyone who has something similar. It's bizarre.

If that isn't strange enough, on my left hand I've been blessed with what is officially called brachydactyly type d.

Remember the hoopla a few years back about the actress Megan Fox's thumb? Yep, that's what I have on my left hand. It's also known as stubby toe thumb, clubbed thumb, stub thumb or hammer thumb. It's quite ridiculous looking if you ask me (feel free to laugh).

It's said that brachydactyly type d is genetic (no one in my family has it so I'm still trying to figure that out) and the only discomfort is the self-consciousness about it. Growing up I would often unconsciously hide my thumb because I was so self-conscious of it.

In college I told people that when I was a young kid my thumb was accidentally chopped off and they couldn't salvage it so they used someone's toe to replace it. My best guy friend in college believed me for over a year and was so upset with me when he found out that I made up that story.

When you don't like something about yourself that you can't change, you can either be miserable about it or laugh about. I choose to laugh about my strange hands and make fun of my toe thumb and extra crease before anyone else does.

Despite my hand's bizarre quirks, I would take having those quirks any day over not having my hands.

day 12: *hands*

Our hands are comprised of 27 bones and two main sets of muscles, the flexor and the extensor muscles. The flexor muscles are connected to the underside of the forearm and bend the fingers and thumbs; the extensor muscles are connected to the top of the forearm and straighten out the fingers and thumbs.

An interesting fact about our hands is that the muscles do not extend into the fingers; it's the action of the muscles on the tendons in the fingers that make the movements.

Our hands are the major tools of our lives—we use them all day long.

They allow us to do things like pick up the children in our lives, eat delicious foods, put on make-up, blow-dry hair, type things on smartphones and computer, turn the steering wheel on a car, feel the touch of a lover's skin, and hundreds of other things that we often take for granted.

Without them we would be dependent on others to do the everyday things that we are so accustomed to doing. The term "hands-on" means "involving or offering active participation rather than theory."

Today, I invite you to be *hands-on* in your practice of gratitude of yourself. Play full out, especially when you are not in the mood to be grateful.

As you go thought your day today, pay special attention to how much you use your hands. Each time you notice them, say, "Thank you"--for your hands and your fingers. Let them know how grateful you are to have them…even if, like me, you have a toe thumb!

day 12: *hands*

it's time to get naked!

morning

1. Set a timer for 1 minute.

Look at yourself naked in the mirror, scanning your body from head to toe, standing in awe of the brilliance that is your body.

2. As you look at yourself naked in the mirror state today's PVS --

I love my hands. I choose to receive all things wonderful with open hands.

3. Focus your attention on your hands. Move your fingers and thumbs around noticing how they move. Notice the lines on your palms, and the skin on the back of your hands.

4. If you wear rings, choose one today that makes your hand feel delicate and lovely.

5. Write down 5 things you are or could be grateful for about your hands.

♥ _____

♥ _____

♥ _____

♥ _____

♥ _____

day 12: *hands*

during the day

At least 6 times today, take a brief moment to notice your hands and all the work they do. Perhaps you can show them a little extra attention today by rubbing coconut oil on them or getting an organic pedicure.

evening

1. At the end of the day review your 5 reasons to be grateful for your hands. Say, "Thank you, thank you, thank you" to your hands and feel the gratitude for the amazingness that is your hands.

2. Before you go to bed, say the PVS one more time and thank your hands for being uniquely yours.

It is only with gratitude that life becomes rich.

Dietrich Bonhoeffer

day 13: *belly - the center of our spirit*

I went to Ethiopia, and it dawned on me that you can tell a starving, malnourished person because they've got a bloated belly and a bald head. And I realized that if you come through any American airport and see businessmen running through with bloated bellies and bald heads, that's malnutrition, too.

Dick Gregory

day 13: *belly*

positive vibration statement
I love my belly. My body is perfect exactly as it is.

day 13: *belly*

If there is one area of the body I hear women complain about the most it's the belly, especially if they've had kids. They will complain about how saggy, fat, filled with stretch marks it is, yet completely miss the fact that under the layer of skin is the entire body's eco-system.

This area that women commonly complain about houses so much goodness. Our stomach, the large and small intestines, our liver, gall bladder, kidneys, adrenals, pancreas, appendix, bladder, ovaries, and fallopian tubes all reside in this area we often disparage. Can you imagine what life would be like without any of these organs?

I don't have to imagine. For many years I experienced what life was like when those organs weren't functioning properly.

Since childhood on I suffered from digestive issues. As a teenager, I was diagnosed as pre-diabetic. Then, at age 20, I lost a child due to birth defects.

I never gave any mind to what the insides of my body needed. I fed my body a diet of processed, refined foods that made my gut completely unhappy. It seemed as if a week didn't go by when I didn't have diarrhea or I wasn't throwing up.

If either of those things weren't happening, I felt like I was about to pass out because my pancreas was producing too much insulin, causing my blood sugar levels to drop due to all of the sugar I ate (which, in turn, caused low-grade depression).

Then, when I became pregnant at 19, my body was so malnourished it wasn't able to feed a growing child.

One would think that with all of those things going on, I would pay more attention to my insides. Nope. Not the case.

For me, it took more than 10 years and getting to a place where I was so depressed and hopeless that I literally wanted to kill myself, before I was able to take all of the greatness stored in my belly area seriously.

day 13: *belly*

I remembered reading about how sugar causes depression so I made a commitment to not eat sugar for a week to see how I felt. I made the commitment to myself that if I felt better I would explore more how food impacts how we feel; and conversely, if I didn't feel better I gave myself permission to end my *miserable* life.

One week of no sugar later, I felt 75% better. I figured I owed it to myself, and to my family, to learn more, so I decided to further explore how food impacts emotions.

Tony Robbins often says, "It is in your moments of decision that your destiny is shaped." In the moment I made the choice to live for one more week, I didn't realize I was changing the course of my life.

From that decision I started to feed myself foods that nourished rather than stole nutrients from me. As my body began to receive much needed nutrients it was finally able to stay in a consistently positive state.

In *Women Food And God*, Geneen Roth stated:

> "The belly is located in the center of our bodies and is in fact the center of our grounding. (Eastern mystics believe the belly is the center of our spirit and that our souls reside there.) Sensing it from the inside—whether it's pulsing or tingling or betraying, whether it's warm or cold or numb—helps us become undeniably and viscerally aware we are alive. We sense the actual physical presence of our life force (by sensing our belly)."

All of life begins in our bellies. The food that we eat is transferred into energy in our intestines. The liver filters our blood that comes from our digestive tract before passing it to the rest of the body.

The kidneys extract waste from blood and balance body fluids.

The ovaries produce eggs so that we can procreate.

The uterus is the perfect house for growing babies.

day 13: *belly*

The belly is the home to so many different organs. It really is a spectacular part of the body.

Today, when you look in the mirror at yourself naked, imagine all of these organs that are under the skin of your belly and express gratitude for everything your belly does for you.

If you want to go a step further, thank it by giving it a delicious salad, veggie soup, or a green smoothie today. It will thank you in return!

day 13: *belly*

it's time to get naked!

morning

1. Set a timer for 1 minute.

Look at yourself naked in the mirror, scanning your body from head to toe, standing in awe of the brilliance that is your body.

2. As you look at yourself naked in the mirror state today's PVS --

I love my belly. My body is perfect exactly as it is.

3. Focus your attention on your belly. Think about how it houses so many different organs that create life for you.

4. Write down 5 things you are or could be grateful for about your belly.

♥ _____

♥ _____

♥ _____

♥ _____

♥ _____

during the day

Each time you eat a meal or a snack today, place your hand on your belly and tell it you love it.

day 13: *belly*

evening

1. At the end of the day review your 5 reasons to be grateful for your belly. Say, "Thank you, thank you, thank you" to your belly and feel the gratitude for the amazingness that is your belly.

2. Before you go to bed, say the PVS one more time and thank your belly for being uniquely yours.

When you arise in the morning think of what a privilege it is to be alive, to think, to enjoy, to love.

Marcus Aurelius

day 13: *belly*

day 14: *our heart has answers*

If you have a heartbeat, there is still time for your dreams.

Sean Stephenson

day 14: *heart*

positive vibration statement

My heart is amazing. I choose to open my heart and allow wonderful things to flow into my life.

day 14: *heart*

I'm guessing, if you are anything like me, you don't think about your heart very often unless you hear about someone having a heart attack. Yet it continues to pump blood to your organs with its faithful and steady beat.

Did you now that only 3 weeks and 1 day after fertilization your heart began to beat?

Beating 100,000 times a day, pumping 1.5 gallons of blood per minute, a woman's average heartbeat is faster than a man's by almost 8 beats a minute.

The heart is truly an amazing organ.

What's even more fascinating about the heart is the fact that scientists believe that our hearts (and other organs) have what is called "cellular memory." Cellular Memory is a theory that our organs store memories or personality traits that remain in the organ and, when transplanted, will be felt and experienced by the recipient.

One case was of a woman, Claire Sylvia, who received a heart and lung transplant in the 1970s from a male donor who was killed in a motorcycle accident. After the surgery Claire reported having intense cravings for beer, chicken nuggets, and green peppers, none of which she enjoyed prior to surgery. Claire's taste for colors changed as well; she went from having pinks as her favorite colors to greens and blues. She even started ogling girls although she had never been attracted to girls previously. You can read Claire's story in her memoir, *A Change of Heart*.

Another interesting story is of a 47-year-old man who, after receiving a heart from a 17-year-old boy, suddenly picked up an intense fondness for classical music. The 17-year-old had been killed in a drive-by shooting, clutching his violin case in his hands.
Some may believe that these stories are far fetched, but I've experienced enough in my life to believe that our hearts do way more than just pump blood.

Recently I heard someone say, "Your head has questions; your heart

day 14: *heart*

has answers." In my own life, and with every client that I've worked with, I've found that when we take time to quiet ourselves, breathe deeply, and listen to the wisdom in our hearts, we always receive the answers we need about love, life, and everything in between.

The HeartMath Institute believes the same thing, as their mission is to "help people bring their physical, mental and emotional systems into balanced alignment with their heart's intuitive guidance." When we get out of our head (where fear resides) and into our hearts (where our intuition and what we know to be true lives), our lives magically begin to shift.

In creating and practicing daily gratitude, which lead me to *28 days naked,* I've personally experienced a shift in my ability to connect deeper to my desires and to no longer tolerate people and experiences in my life who do not serve who I am or what I want for my life. I believe the same will happen for you as well if you do the practice.

According to the HeartMath Institute "an effective way to improve mental, emotional, physical and spiritual well-being is to invoke and sustain sincere appreciation. The greater your capacity for sincere appreciate, the deeper the connection to your heart, where intuition and unlimited inspiration and possibilities reside." This is my desire for you.

As you shower your body with appreciation and love you will continue to connect with the deepest part of yourself so that you may live a life of intuition, vibrant energy and inspiration.

Today, as you look at yourself naked, place your hand over your heart. Take a moment to breath deeply into your heart for 5 breaths as you look at yourself and say "thank you" with each inhale. After 5 breaths, thank your heart for the amazing job it does every day for you.

Set a couple of alarms throughout the day to remind yourself to express gratitude for your heart. After you settle into your bed, place your hand on your heart again and thank it before you go to sleep. As your heart experiences appreciation and gratitude it will continue to grow into a heart of gratitude. And that's where the fun begins!

day 14: *heart*

it's time to get naked!

morning

1. Set a timer for 1 minute.

Look at yourself naked in the mirror, scanning your body from head to toe, standing in awe of the brilliance that is your body.

2. As you look at yourself naked in the mirror state today's PVS --

My heart is amazing. I choose to open my heart and allow wonderful things to flow into my life.

3. Focus your attention on the area where your heart resides. Put your hands over your heart and with each inhalation and exhalation feel your heartbeat. Notice how peaceful and steady it is as you breathe deeply.

4. Write down 5 things you are or could be grateful for about your heart.

♥ _____

♥ _____

♥ _____

♥ _____

♥ _____

day 14: *heart*

during the day

At least half a dozen times today (set reminders on your phone, if necessary), place your hands over your heart and say, "I choose to open my heart today" (setting a reminder on your phone is a great way to remember to do this).

evening

1. At the end of the day review your 5 reasons to be grateful for your heart. Say, "Thank you, thank you, thank you" to your heart and feel the gratitude for the amazingness that is your heart

2. Before you go to bed, say the PVS one more time and thank your heart for being uniquely yours.

Gratitude is the memory of the heart.

Jean-Baptiste Massieu

day 15: *the brain that changes itself*

It's our hearts and brains that we should exercise more often. You can put on all the makeup you want, but it won't make your soul pretty.

Kevyn Aucoin

day 15: *brain*

positive vibration statement

My brain is absolutely incredible. I fill my mind with positive beliefs and thoughts that create a life I love.

day 15: *brain*

Growing up there was a general thought that no matter how you were, you would always be that way and there was no way of changing. I was taught to believe that the thoughts I had were to be believed as gospel and never to be questioned.

At sixteen, after passing out on our back porch when my sister was giving me a perm (yes, I said a perm. Remember when those were cool? If you don't, be grateful for that!) my dad took me to the hospital and I was diagnosed with pre-diabetes. The doctor said, "Just don't eat sugar and you'll be fine." Gee, thanks, that's not so helpful to a 16-year-old in America!

Most of my teens and twenties were spent living in a world of negative thoughts, depressive emotions, and the thought of killing myself. My blood sugar levels were consistently low which generally made me live in a state of annoyance, anger, and frustration. To say that I wasn't the most pleasant person to be around is an understatement. It was as if I was the female version of the Incredible Hulk—my moods shifted in an instant.

I remember my college boyfriend telling me--whenever I would turn into my angry state--that I could choose how I felt. As you can imagine, my response was not pleasant. I'd typically yell at him, asking if he really thought that I would purposely choose to feel angry. Those conversations never went well.

Flash forward to when I was 31, absolutely miserable, hating my life, and completely directionless. There was a 24-hour period where I didn't get out of bed. In that 24-hour period I thought of 5 different ways to end my life that all sounded like great ideas. I knew logically that taking my life was not a good idea, but I felt life would always be terrible for me, so what was the point of living?

In an instant, I remembered something I had read that talked about how sugar causes depression. I didn't want to leave the legacy of an aunt who killed herself to my nieces and nephews. So, as I mentioned in day 13— the belly, I made a deal with myself to not eat sugar for a week to see if it would change anything. If I felt better I would explore the idea that food makes us feel certain ways emotionally. If

day 15: *brain*

I didn't feel better I gave myself permission to end my life. Dramatic? Yes. But, that was my reality at the time.

That one decision started my journey into understanding that my college boyfriend was right--I actually do have a choice in how I feel. (Don't you hate it when others are right?). One week of no sugar literally changed my entire life.

Since that day I have been immersed in learning how I can change my life through changing my brain. I've learned that what I eat, my lifestyle, and the thoughts that I focus on all have a huge impact on the quality of my moods.

As I have chosen foods and thoughts that support how I want to feel, I now live in a world of positive thoughts, happy emotions, and a desire to live.

To be completely transparent, there are times when the negative emotions surface (I am human after all). The difference is that now I know I have a choice in how I feel. I have the ability to explore what's causing the negative state by asking myself questions: What did I eat? Did I get enough sleep? Does my body need exercise? What I am focusing on?

Our brains are beyond amazing. The belief I had growing up that there is no way people can change how we think is complete bullsh*t. When you take back the control of your mind and realize that you are not your thoughts, then you harness the amazing power we are all born with--neuroplasticity, the brain's ability to change itself, reverse negative thinking patterns, and operate at a level of clarity you have always desired.

What we eat, how much (or little) we exercise, the amount and quality of sleep we get, and how often we express gratitude makes a profound impact on our brains.

Study after study reveals that those who have higher levels of gratitude experience better sleep and lower levels of anxiety and depression. Gratitude literally makes you happier, healthier, and sexier.

day 15: *brain*

Books like Dr. Amen's *Change Your Brain, Change Your Life* and Norman Doidge's *The Brain That Changes Itself: Stories of Personal Triumph From The Frontier's of Brain Science* tell us story after story of how we can transform our lives from living in a place of sadness, anger, and frustration to living in a place of positive thoughts, happy emotions, and a desire to live.

It begins first with gratitude.

There's an old saying, "If you've forgotten the language of gratitude, you'll never be on speaking terms with happiness."

Today, I invite you to set an alarm on your phone to go off each hour to remind you to express gratitude. First, for your brain that has the ability to change when given the things it needs.

Second, express gratitude for the fact that you woke up today. Hundreds of thousand of people cannot say the same about their loved ones. Today is the only day that you will ever have that is like this one. Thank God, the Universe, whomever you believe in for waking up and expect that today is your day to shine.

Third, express gratitude that you now know that you do have a choice in how you feel. You are no longer the victim of your thoughts and emotions. You now know you have the ability to choose negative or positive thoughts. That is freedom.

As you go to bed tonight, thank your brain for everything it has done for you that you aren't even aware of. Then, when you wake up tomorrow notice how going to sleep in a state of gratitude has the power to change your life.

day 15: *brain*

it's time to get naked!

morning

1. Set a timer for 1 minute.

Look at yourself naked in the mirror, scanning your body from head to toe, standing in awe of the brilliance that is your body.

2. As you look at yourself naked in the mirror state today's PVS --

My brain is absolutely incredible. I fill my mind with positive beliefs and thoughts that create a life I love.

3. Focus your attention on your head, imagining what your brain looks like.

4. Write down 5 things you are or could be grateful for about your brain.

♥ _____

♥ _____

♥ _____

♥ _____

♥ _____

day 15: *brain*

during the day

Today set your alarms as stated above and express gratitude throughout the day.

Notice your thoughts. When you have a thought that seems negative, be curious and observe it. Ask yourself if the thought is really true. Ask yourself who you would be without the thought.

When you have a positive thought, express gratitude for it.

When you change a thought, express gratitude for the ability to change your focus to something more positive.

evening

1. At the end of the day review your 5 reasons to be grateful for your brain. Say, "Thank you, thank you, thank you" to your brain and feel the gratitude for the amazingness that is your brain.

2. Before you go to bed, say the PVS one more time and thank your brain for being uniquely yours.

He is a wise man who does not grieve for those things which he has not, but rejoices for those which he has.

Epictetus

day 15: *brain*

day 16: *hips don't lie*

I'm fine, and my hips are fine. My false knee is fine. My false hips are fine. Everything's cooking.

Liza Minnelli

day 16: *hips*

positive vibration statement
I love my hips. They carry me through life with ease and joy.

day 16: *hips*

One of my favorite memories of my maternal grandmother is from when I was about seven years old. My mom and I were visiting her at her home in California for a week; I have no idea where my mom was at the time, but I remember as my grand-mom put me to bed one night, she dressed up in her belly dancing costume and belly-danced for me.

As I watched her I was enthralled at her ability to move her hips. I remember thinking how free she seemed, how playful her energy was and how much she laughed. The control she had over the movements of her hips was memorizing.

At the time I didn't know the words, but now I can say that my grandmother was, in that moment, living 100% in her feminine energy. And I knew then and there that I wanted to be like that.

Flash forward to a few years later when it was time to start going to school dances. I soon learned that I may have inherited my grandmother's sense of adventure, but I did not inherit her ability to move. I can't move my hips, I can't move my feet. I am so white with two left feet it isn't funny. When I dance the words "free" and "playful" are not adjectives one would use to describe me.

If you've ever seen *16 Candles*, think of the scene at the school dance with Joan Cusack dancing while wearing her neck-brace. That's what I feel like when I dance. Awkward.

As we all do at times, especially as teenagers, we give meaning to things that aren't necessarily true. Because I didn't have the ability to dance and move my hips the way my grandmother did—free and playful—I decided that it must mean that I was not feminine. For years I wrestled with this, consistently feeling "not enough." My model of the world was *femininity = the ability to shake one's hips in a fun and playful way*.

Since my outside world did not match up with my inside ideas of what the world "should be," I spent many sad and miserable nights by myself.

day 16: *hips*

As I've matured I've learned that femininity can be expressed in many ways, not just through dance. I learned that the ability to receive compliments and assistance, the ability to just "be" rather than to always focus on the next accomplishment, and to feel and express my emotions makes me just as feminine as dancing made my grandmother. I also learned that not everyone was born dancing and that it's a skill I can learn.

As a woman, we've been gifted hips that miraculously expand and give birth to life. Our bodies are absolutely astounding. That God, nature, whatever you want to believe in created our hips in such a way that they function perfectly to create and bring new life through birth is beyond belief.

Yet, we often get so caught up in judging and comparing ourselves and how our body looks and functions with other women ("My hips are too big"; "I can't move my hips like that") that we completely lose sight of how divinely feminine we are.

We lose sight of the fact that the hips that we have been given are amazingly feminine and have the capacity to create and carry so much life in them. They are the hips that nature intended YOU to have.

Before writing this I thought I should get more in touch with my hips, so I pulled up Shakira's *Hips Don't Lie* video on YouTube and attempted to shake my hips along with her.

Sadly, I still haven't mastered the art of moving my hips the way she or my grand mom can. What I have mastered is the ability to laugh at myself in the process, which is a far cry from judging and criticizing myself. That non-judgmental laughter came from practicing gratitude for every part of my body, including my white girl hips.

As we wrap up today, take a moment to place your hands on your hips. Take a deep breath in and allow yourself to feel everything that goes on in-between your hips. According to the Chakra system, between our hips lie the ability for creativity, passion, orgasm, (yes, please) and, if it's meant to be for you, giving birth to another life.

day 16: *hips*

Today, as you walk, place your hands on your hips and allow yourself to feel your hips rise and fall. Express gratitude for your hips with each step you take, each stair you climb. When you lay down to go to sleep, place your hands on your hips and let them know how grateful you are for all they have done for you today. Fall asleep knowing that every night your hips "don't lie" as they are yet another reminder that you are absolutely Divine!

day 16: *hips*

it's time to get naked!

morning

1. Set a timer for 1 minute.

Look at yourself naked in the mirror, scanning your body from head to toe, standing in awe of the brilliance that is your body.

2. As you look at yourself naked in the mirror state today's PVS --

I love my hips. They carry me through life with ease and joy.

3. Focus your attention on your hips. Place your hands on them as if you were Wonder Woman and feel the power that lies in your hips.

4. Write down 5 things you are or could be grateful for about your hips.

♥ _____

♥ _____

♥ _____

♥ _____

♥ _____

during the day

As you walk today, notice the swing in your hips and smile with gratitude.

day 16: *hips*

evening

1. At the end of the day review your 5 reasons to be grateful for your hips. Say, "Thank you, thank you, thank you" to your hips and feel the gratitude for the amazingness of your hips.

2. Before you go to bed, say the PVS one more time and thank your hips for being uniquely yours.

The discipline of gratitude is the explicit effort to acknowledge that all I am and have is given to me as a gift of love, a gift to be celebrated with joy.

Henri Nouwen

day 16: *hips*

day 17: *i love my thighs*

If you are ever wondering, 'If I have thinner thighs and shinier hair will I be happier?' you just need to meet a group of models because they have the thinnest thighs and the shiniest hair and the coolest clothes and they're the most physically insecure women on the planet.

Cameron Russell

day 17: *thighs*

positive vibration statement
I love my thighs. They confidently move me forward into a bright future.

day 17: *thighs*

Take a look down at your thighs. What do you see? What feelings come up for you as you look at them?

Do you see thighs that have taken you places and allowed you to have amazing experiences or do you see flesh that you loathe?

Do you experience joy when you look at your thighs or do you experience disgust?

As women we all have certain places on our bodies we'd love to change. For many women, it's their thighs, as evidenced by statements like, "My thighs are too fat," "I wish my thighs didn't touch," or "I have thunder thighs." I don't think I've ever heard another woman express that she loves her thighs.

The thighbone (aka your femur) is the longest and strongest bone in the body. It's really a shame that our thighs don't receive the love they deserve, because we tend to look at everything surrounding the bone and wish that most of it wasn't there.

There is one woman I know of that has never complained about her thighs, Jen Bricker. If you've never heard of Jen Bricker, you HAVE to Google her.

Jen was born without out legs to Romanian parents who gave her up at birth. Adopted by an American couple living in a small town in Illinois, Jen's adoptive parents raised her to believe that *can't* was a 4-letter word. Jen's parents deeply loved and accepted her and encouraged her to pursue her dreams. Jen grew up playing volleyball, softball, and basketball, but her true love was gymnastics.

Jen was a natural at power tumbling winning state titles and competed in the Junior Olympics. Whenever it was pointed out to Jen how good she was at tumbling despite the fact that she was handicapped and needed to use a wheelchair, Jen would explain that the wheelchair was just to keep her from getting dirty. Talk about an amazing attitude!

day 17: *thighs*

I'm sure many people wouldn't blame Jen if she decided to be bitter about not having legs, but her parents would not allow her to have that kind of thinking.

Since *can't* has never been a word Jen used, she has, according to her website, become a professional acrobat and aerialist who has traveled internationally with Britney Spears' World Tour, appeared as a headliner at the Palazzo Hotel in Las Vegas, Lincoln Center in New York City, and The Shangri La Hotel in Dubai. She's been featured in shows such as *20/20*, *Good Morning America* and *HBO Real Sports*. In addition to those accomplishments, Jen is also a worldwide speaker.

As if that doesn't make for an amazing story, Jen's story gets even better. Her childhood idol was the 1996 gymnastic gold-medalist Dominique Moceanu. Jen never asked about her adoption until she was 16 years old. That's when she learned that Dominique was her older biological sister, and, that Dominique didn't know about her. Jen eventually met her biological family and formed a relationship with Dominque. If you want to know more, Jen's story is chronicled in Dominique Moceanu's book *Off Balance*.

In 2014 I had the privilege of meeting Jen and hearing her speak at a training event. Jen's presence, joy, and gratitude filled the room. She never cursed her thighs because she doesn't have them. And, she chose to not curse the fact that she doesn't have thighs.

Jen Bricker's mission is to inspire and motivate others to believe that anything is truly possible. And that, my smart, sexy friend, is my desire for you.

Through covering your body with love and gratitude I hope that you will begin to believe that anything truly is possible. By expressing gratitude daily for the body you've been given, it is possible to cultivate a healthy body image.

I hope that by sharing Jen's story with you, I have inspired you to look at your thighs and say, "I love my thighs" knowing all the ways they support you. Each time you stand or sit today, thank your quadriceps

day 17: *thighs*

for consistently serving you without you having to consciously ask them to. As you walk, thank each femur for its strength.

When you are sitting in a manner that may normally make you curse your thighs, thank them for being YOUR thighs and for being a part of YOUR legs that have the ability to move you forward as you choose!

day 17: *thighs*

it's time to get naked!

morning

1. Set a timer for 1 minute.

Look at yourself naked in the mirror, scanning your body from head to toe, standing in awe of the brilliance that is your body.

2. As you look at yourself naked in the mirror state today's PVS --

I love my thighs. They confidently move me forward into a bright future.

3. Focus your attention on your thighs. Acknowledge the strength your thighs have that allows you to stand up and sit down.

4. Write down 5 things you are or could be grateful for about your thighs.

♥ _____

♥ _____

♥ _____

♥ _____

♥ _____

day 17: *thighs*

during the day

Whenever you sit down or stand up today, thank your thighs for their strength and power. Also, as you walk, express gratitude to your thighs for moving your forward.

evening

1. At the end of the day review your 5 reasons to be grateful for your thighs. Say, "Thank you, thank you, thank you" to your thighs and feel the gratitude for the amazingness that is your thighs.

2. Before you go to bed, say the PVS one more time and thank your thighs for being uniquely yours.

Gratitude is not only the greatest of virtues, but the parent of all the others.

Marcus Tullius Cicero

day 17: *thighs*

day 18: *on bended knee*

I don't want to sound like a Hallmark card, but to be able to wake up each day with food and shelter, that alone is good. Forget aging and the fact that my butt is becoming a little more familiar with my knees than my tailbone. If you are six feet above ground it's a good day. So, give me more!

Faith Hill

day 18: *knees*

positive vibration statement
My knees are amazing. They bend and support me with ease and grace.

day 18: *knees*

Growing up my younger brother Justin and I used to make fun of our dad whenever he walked up the stairs. His knees would make a clicking sound that my brother would imitate by snapping his fingers when my dad walked up the stairs. Justin and I would crack up laughing, and my dad would yell at us, "It's not funny!" (We disagreed; it was very funny).

We assumed that his knees made the sound because he was "old" (because to kids, anyone above 30 was old). I eventually learned was that his knees made that noise because his body wasn't getting the right nutrients.

Once he changed his diet and eliminated the foods that caused inflammation in his body (for him that was sugar, dairy, and gluten) his knees stopped clicking. Great news for him. As for my brother and I, we had to find other things to tease him about.

Our culture has taught us that it's "normal" for our joints to start creaking at a certain age. My belief is that is not true. How we age depends on how well we nurture ourselves. If one part of our body is imbalanced, another part is as well.

In Chinese medicine when there is knee difficulty, it is an indication that there is a kidney function disorder. Conversely, if you have healthy kidneys, you won't experience knee problems. (This, of course, does not include trauma to the knees).

In spiritual practices, the knees are believed to represent pride and where we assimilate knowledge and learning. "Taking a knee" or kneeling is showing respect, honor, and surrender. It's said that this is why we kneel when we receive things, such as healing or being knighted.

It's why people kneel when they pray and why men get on one knee to propose.

When we are unwilling or unable to bend at the knee, it indicates being inflexible and stuck in the ego. What's more fascinating to me about

day 18: *knees*

this way of thinking is that the knee is considered the largest and most complex joint in the body.

It seems logical that the most complex joint in our bodies would be connected to one of the most complex parts of who we are—our ego. Emotions of pride, respect, honor, and surrender are not easy emotions to understand.

From a structural standpoint, the three bones that make up the knee--the femur (the thigh bone), the tibia (the shin bone) and the kneecap (patella)--bear a force equivalent to three to six times the body's weight with each step you take.

That means that if you weigh 140 pounds your knees are taking a 420-pound or more beating with every step. The average sedentary person walks, on average 1,000-3,000 steps a day (an active person generally walks 8,000-10,000 steps per day). If we were to use the numbers of a sedentary person and multiply 420 pounds by 3,000 that would be 1,260,000 pounds of weight per day that each knee bears. Amazing.

As you read this, place your hand on one of your knees. Bend it back and forth. Feel your kneecap, your muscles and your ligaments. Think about how utterly amazing it is that your largest and most complex joint bears your weight all day and thank it.

With each step you take today, thank your knees for how they carry your weight and the weight of everything you lift.

Tonight, before you go to bed, do something different. Kneel beside your bed and give thanks for the work your knees did for you today as well as this the amazing body you have. Your knees, and your kidneys, will love you in return.

day 18: *knees*

it's time to get naked!

morning

1. Set a timer for 1 minute.

Look at yourself naked in the mirror, scanning your body from head to toe, standing in awe of the brilliance that is your body.

2. As you look at yourself naked in the mirror state today's PVS --

My knees are amazing. They bend and support me with ease and grace.

3. Focus your attention on your knees. Look at them from the front, side, and back. Thank them for how they carry you throughout the day.

4. Write down 5 things you are or could be grateful for about your knees.

♥ _____

♥ _____

♥ _____

♥ _____

♥ _____

day 18: *knees*

during the day

Whenever your stand up, sit down, or bend today, thank your knees for their support and grace.

evening

1. At the end of the day review your 5 reasons to be grateful for your knees. Say, "Thank you, thank you, thank you" to your knees and feel the gratitude for the amazingness that is your knees.

2. Before you go to bed, kneel beside your bed, say the PVS one more time and give thanks for the work your knees did for today.

> Acknowledging the good that you already have in your life is the foundation for all abundance.
>
> Eckhart Tolle

day 19: *sexy calves*

I had to grow to love my body. I did not have a good self-image at first. Finally it occurred to me, I'm either going to love me or hate me. And I chose to love myself. Then everything kind of sprung from there. Things that I thought weren't attractive became sexy. Confidence makes you sexy.

Queen Latifah

day 19: *calves*

positive vibration statement

I love my calves. I appreciate all of the movements my body performs.

day 19: *calves*

Do you love to wear heels? It seems as though women either love them or hate them—there's no in-between.

Me? I fall into the "hate" category. I've had so many issues with my body's alignment that wearing heels has always been ridiculously painful for me. Two steps and—bam--my back goes out of alignment. Not so fun when you want to get all dolled up!

Despite my pain in them, I can totally understand the allure of wearing high heels. They may be painful for some of us, but there is no arguing that they make our legs look sexier!

Today, I want to focus on the calf muscles because, as women, our legs are one of the body parts that we pay a lot of attention to and we unconsciously show off.

We wear heels because we subconsciously associate high heels with femininity and attractiveness. Feeling attractive often equates to a feeling of power. We wear high heels because they show off our calf muscles. We wear them because they can make our legs look longer and leaner.

As a human, our body weight is supported on two limbs instead of 4, like most other animals. Compared to other animals, we have exceptionally large calf muscles, yet as women, that's not something we necessarily take as a compliment (we'll take big boobs but not big calves).

Our calf muscles are a group of seven muscles in the lower part of the leg separated into two groups, superficial and deep.

The superficial group is the two bulges of muscle that people think of when they think of calves. These muscles are used for running and jumping as well as steadying your legs when standing. These are the muscles that you are enhancing when you wear heels.

The deep group is the set of muscles that do things we rarely think about consciously, like flexing the toes and supporting the arch of the foot.

day 19: *calves*

Without these seven muscles, everyday actions such as standing, slipping your foot inside your shoe, and walking would be incredibly difficult. If you've ever had a calf strain, you know what I mean.

If you are sitting down reading this, when you stand up, thank you calf muscles for helping you steady your legs.

If you are slipping a pair of heels on (or any shoe for that matter), take a look at your legs and, with a big smile on your face, think, "Wow, my calf muscles are so sexy."

If you drive today, think about how your calf muscles allow you to press on the gas and the brake.

As you go throughout the day, with every step, with every shoe change, every time you flex your feet, thank your calf muscles for allowing you to do those actions.

When you crawl into bed tonight, think about everything you did today and how your calves played a key role in each of them. Your calves will be glad you did!

day 19: *calves*

it's time to get naked!

morning

1. Set a timer for 1 minute.

Look at yourself naked in the mirror, scanning your body from head to toe, standing in awe of the brilliance that is your body.

2. As you look at yourself naked in the mirror state today's PVS --

I love my calves. I appreciate all of the movements my body performs.

3. Focus your attention on your calves. Check them out standing on flat feet, then flex your feet and look at them. Thank them for how easy they make it for you to stand up, steady your legs, and jump.

4. Write down 5 things you are or could be grateful for about your calves.

♥ _____

♥ _____

♥ _____

♥ _____

♥ _____

day 19: *calves*

during the day

As you walk today, thank your calves for their strength and power.

evening

1. At the end of the day review your 5 reasons to be grateful for your calves. Say, "Thank you, thank you, thank you" to your calves and feel the gratitude for the amazingness of your calves.

2. Before you go to bed, say the PVS one more time and thank your calves for being uniquely yours.

If a fellow isn't thankful for what he's got, he isn't likely to be thankful for what he's going to get.

Frank A. Clark

day 20: *jump in with both feet*

Forget not that the earth delights to feel your bare feet and the winds long to play with your hair.

Khalil Gibran

day 20: *feet*

positive vibration statement
I love my feet. My feet take me to new and wonderful places.

day 20: *feet*

Today is all about putting your best foot forward!

On day 18, I alluded to daily steps. If you are a moderately active person, you take about 7,500 steps per day. If you run or jump on a mini-trampoline (one of my favorite forms of exercise), you probably take about 10,000 steps per day. And, you probably take all these steps without thinking about putting one foot in front of the other or about how much work your feet do.

The funny thing about feet is that some people are completely repulsed by feet while other people are totally turned on by them. (Ever heard of people with foot fetishes?)

If you are barefoot right now or are in a place where you can easily take off your shoes, take a look at your feet. If not, just imagine your feet. Love them or hate them, they are pretty amazing. With 26 bones, 33 joints, more than 100 tendons, muscles, and ligaments, plus a whopping 250,000 sweat glands, the foot does an amazing job of supporting your entire body while keeping you balanced and safe.

The completely amazing thing about the foot is that there are over 7,000 nerve endings that we call reflexes that correspond to every organ and system within the body.

The skin on the palms of your feet (your arches) is the thickest skin on your body, followed by the soles (ball and heel) of your feet. Yet, according to reflexology, if these reflex points are touched with pressure or therapeutic grade essential oils are applied, then the nervous system corresponding to that particular area of the foot is stimulated and blocked or congested energy pathways can open up and healing can begin.

For example, if you feel a headache coming on, make small circles with your thumbs on the underside of your big toes. Reflexology states that this area on your toe is connected to your head and your neck, so the rubbing motion will relieve your headache.

Every day, right after I get out of the shower, while my pores are the most open, my favorite thing to support having a positive mindset is to

day 20: *feet*

put Bergamot essential oil on my big toes. Since I've been doing that I've noticed a decrease in my negative mindset. It doesn't totally make sense to me that I can be happier just by putting an essential oil on my big toe, but it works.

Think about the last time someone massaged your feet. Remember how after a five or ten minute foot rub, you had the energy to last throughout the rest of the day. Our whole being feels reinvigorated in a different way when someone rubs our feet than when someone rubs a part of our leg or arm.

Your feet have exceptional powers to create health in the rest of your body. As you give them the much-needed love and gratitude they deserve, you'll start to see that the rest of your body will also feel loved and cherished.

Let's jump in with both feet to practice gratitude for your feet and your entire body today. Let's get you moving further and faster towards a body and life you love by living in a space of gratitude for the all of the bones, joints, ligaments, and muscles that make up your feet.

If you are one of the people who are repulsed by feet and find little to be grateful for, here are a few of my favorites:

- ♥ I'm grateful for how my feet absorb each shock of each step.

- ♥ I'm grateful for the balance my feet give me which allow me to stand upright.

- ♥ I'm grateful that my toenail polish can last weeks on my toes.

- ♥ I'm grateful that I have hundreds of different ways to show off my feet

- ♥ With each step you take today say, "Thank you, thank you, thank you" to your feet.

If you stub your toe, express gratitude that you have toes to feel pain. If, at the end of the day, your feet are killing you because you've been

day 20: *feet*

in heels all day, express gratitude that you have the opportunity to put on a comfy pair of shoes.

It's a great day to let your feet feel loved and cherished!

day 20: *feet*

it's time to get naked!

morning

1. Set a timer for 1 minute.

Look at yourself naked in the mirror, scanning your body from head to toe, standing in awe of the brilliance that is your body.

2. As you look at yourself naked in the mirror state today's PVS --

I love my feet.
My feet take me to new and wonderful places.

3. Focus your attention on your feet. Curiously look at your ankles and toes as well as the tops and bottoms of your feet. Thank them for allowing you to walk from your bed to your mirror and for all the walking they will do today.

4. Write down 5 things you are or could be grateful for about your feet.

♥ _____

♥ _____

♥ _____

♥ _____

♥ _____

day 20: *feet*

during the day

As you walk today, thank your feet for all the work they do for you each day.

evening

1. At the end of the day review your 5 reasons to be grateful for your feet. Say, "Thank you, thank you, thank you" to your feet and feel the gratitude for the amazingness of your feet.

2. Before you go to bed, say the PVS one more time and thank your feet for being uniquely yours.

If you want to turn your life around, try thankfulness. It will change your life mightily.

Gerald Good

day 20: *feet*

day 21: *comfortable in your own skin*

Glamour is about feeling good in your own skin.

Zoe Saldana

day 21: *skin*

positive vibration statement

My skin is amazing. I am grateful for all the ways I feel and experience life.

day 21: *skin*

Today is all about our largest detox organ, our skin. Take a look at the top of your hands. What do you notice about your skin?

Is it smooth or wrinkled? Is the color fair or dark? Do you have freckles or is it spotless?

I've always been a fair-skinned, freckled girl who hated this about herself. Growing up I thought that my freckles made me look boyish and that my fair skin was a sure sign that I was definitely ugly (I have no idea where I came up with that).

In my 20s I didn't like my skin because it was so dry all the time. My elbows were always so dry that they would snag on clothes (isn't that such a gross feeling?).

Looking back at pictures of myself, I now see that I was an adorable kid (except for the phase when my mom had my hair cut short and I had braces-- that was just awkward). Those freckles and fair skin made up so much of who I was then and who I have become now. I now know the texture of my skin is up to me and I can change that by what I eat and drink as well as by what I put on my skin.

Your skin is not only your largest detox organ, but it is also your largest organ overall. Making up for about 15% of your body weight, your skin sheds over 30,000 dead cells per minute. That's right, 30,000 per minute!

What that really means is that 50% of the dust in your home is actually dead skin (kind of gross when you think about it, eh?).

Every 28 days your skin completely renews itself. The skin you are looking at today is not the same skin you saw 28 days ago.

If you have skin challenges, such as dry skin, acne, or eczema, you literally have the ability to change how your skin looks in 28 days simply by changing what you put into and on your body. Take a moment to imagine how healthy your skin can be just 28 short days from now.

day 21: *skin*

In addition to the practice of gratitude, your skin will get a healthy glow from a few other things you can easily give it.

One simple thing is water—our skin craves water. If you commit, for the next 28 days, to drink warm water with lemon in the morning and then water throughout the rest of the day you will absolutely notice a positive difference in your skin. It will be softer, smoother, and it will glow.

Another simple thing you can do to give your skin that healthy glow is to feed your body more vegetables and fruits while decreasing the amount of processed foods, dairy and sugar.

Most women don't realize that sugar ages us faster than nature intended. Collagen and elastin, two protein fibers that keep our skin firm and supple, are damaged with each bite of sugar we consume. When we eat sugar, we trigger a process called Glycation to begin.

In this process, the sugar in the bloodstream attaches to the collagen and elastin, creating harmful new molecules called Advance Glycation End products, or AGEs (aptly named, eh).

The more sugar you eat the more AGEs you develop. The more AGEs you develop the more your skin ages. Dull, sagging, and wrinkled skin is the result. Eating sugar literally makes you look older than you are.

Dairy can have the opposite effect in that it can produce pimples, making you feel like you are a teenager again (I'm guessing that's not the "younger" look you are going for).

If you have skin issues like dry skin, acne or eczema, remember that your skin is your largest detox organ. When you see things on your skin that you know shouldn't be there, it's because your body is trying to get it something it doesn't like out of its system.

Start to pay attention to what you are eating. Keep a food journal to track what is going in so you can see if it is connected to what's coming out of you, through your skin (remember, issues such as dry

day 21: *skin*

skin, acne & eczema are all examples of this). Experiment with adding in or subtracting some foods to see what allows you to be the most comfortable in your own skin.

As you go throughout the day today, each time you get a glimpse of your skin, send it some love and gratitude for how it protects your bones and organs. Let it know that you are grateful for it's color, elasticity, and even the freckles or "blemishes" that you once didn't like, as they are all of the amazing things that make up exactly who you are!

day 21: *skin*

it's time to get naked!

morning

1. Set a timer for 1 minute.

Look at yourself naked in the mirror, scanning your body from head to toe, standing in awe of the brilliance that is your body.

2. As you look at yourself naked in the mirror state today's PVS --

My skin is amazing. I am grateful for all the ways I feel and experience life.

3. Focus your attention on your skin. Notice its color, elasticity, and all of the different "blemishes" that make up your skin. Thank your skin for protecting your bones and organs as well as for its ability to change.

4. Write down 5 things you are or could be grateful for about your skin.

♥ _____

♥ _____

♥ _____

♥ _____

♥ _____

day 21: *skin*

during the day

Whenever you catch a glimpse of your skin today, send it some love and gratitude for its protection.

Whenever something touches your skin today, notice it and thank your skin for the sensation.

evening

1. At the end of the day review your 5 reasons to be grateful for your skin. Say, "Thank you, thank you, thank you" to your skin and feel the gratitude for the amazingness that is your skin.

2. Before you go to bed, say the PVS one more time and thank your skin for being uniquely yours.

Gratitude is a currency that we can mint for ourselves, and spend without fear of bankruptcy.

Fred De Witt Van Amburgh

day 21: *skin*

day 22: *shake your booty*

God made a very obvious choice when he made me voluptuous; why would I go against what he decided for me? My limbs work, so I'm not going to complain about the way my body is shaped.

Drew Barrymore

day 22: *booty*

positive vibration statement
I love my booty. I am whole, complete, and full of vibrant energy.

day 22: *booty*

If you grew up in the 90s you certainly remember the beginning of Sir Mix A-Lot's *Baby Got Back.*

> Oh. My. God,
> Becky, look at her butt
> It's so big
> She looks like one of those rap guys' girlfriends
> Who understands those rap guys
> They only talk to her because she looks like a total prostitute
> I mean, her butt
> It's just so big....

I remember singing along to this with my one of my high school best friends and cracking up while we were singing. I also remember having times growing up when I wondered if I had a *good* butt. Was it too big? Or was it too small?

For most of my 20s I earned my living as a waitress. I worked in environments with sports playing on the televisions, which meant there were lots of guys around.

After I started paying attention to what guys were saying to me I realized that my butt was never going to be *right* for every guy.

One of the guys I worked with was Puerto Rican and he said that as a Puerto Rican he likes his girls with some fat. He told me that my butt was too small, so I actually thought I needed to work on making my butt bigger.

Then a white guy who liked really petite girls told me that my butt wasn't tiny enough, so then thought I needed to work on shrinking my butt. Would my butt ever be *just right*?

I realized the answer was Yes and No.

Fact is—one guy is going to love that you have a big butt, another won't. One guy will love that you don't have a big butt, another won't.

But none of that matters until <u>you</u> are content with what you have.

day 22: *booty*

That may mean that you know you are carrying a bit more "junk in the trunk" than your body can handle, and it's time to get moving.

Or, it could mean that you know your glutes have the ability to be more toned than they currently are, and it's time to get moving.

I'm sure that there may be some things that you cannot change about your butt, but if you have the ability to move then you have the ability to do squats, go for a walk or run, do yoga, ride a bike, or do any other kind of activity that gives you control over the size of your butt.

Either way, you don't get the butt you want by sitting on it. Get up and do something about it. As KC and the Sunshine Band sang, *(Shake, Shake, Shake) Shake Your Booty*. And, while you're shaking it, express gratitude that for the butt that you've been given and for the ability to shake it. (Even if, like me, you're not the best at shaking what your momma gave you, you still have it to shake it.)

In addition to the daily exercise today, every time you sit or stand, say a quick "thank you" to your butt. Without it, it would be really challenging to sit or stand. If you follow these steps, before you know it, you may have the butt you've always wanted!

day 22: *booty*

it's time to get naked!

morning

1. Set a timer for 1 minute.

Look at yourself naked in the mirror, scanning your body from head to toe, standing in awe of the brilliance that is your body.

2. As you look at yourself naked in the mirror state today's PVS --

I love my booty. I am whole, complete, and full of vibrant energy.

3. Focus your attention on your booty. Check it out from the back and side view and thank it for being your booty. Thank it for how it cushions you when you sit and for how you have the ability to change it if you choose to.

4. Write down 5 things you are or could be grateful for about your booty.

♥ _____

♥ _____

♥ _____

♥ _____

♥ _____

day 22: *booty*

during the day

Whenever you sit, thank your butt for cushioning your bones.

Whenever you sit or stand, thank your butt for helping you to do so.

evening

1. At the end of the day review your 5 reasons to be grateful for your butt. Say, "Thank you, thank you, thank you" to your butt and feel the gratitude for the amazingness that is your butt.

2. Before you go to bed, say the PVS one more time and thank your butt for being uniquely yours.

The way to develop the best that is in a person is by appreciation and encouragement.

Charles Schwab

day 23: *feel it in your bones*

Embrace and love your body. It's the most amazing thing you will ever own.

Unknown

day 23: *bones*

positive vibration statement

I love my bones. My strong, healthy bones support me through every stage of my life.

day 23: *bones*

Have you ever broken a bone? If so, do you remember what it was like to experience life with the cast on? Not being able to do the things that you loved as easily?

When I was eight I had a bike accident that caused me to break both of my arms. The doctors had to put me to sleep to pop my right wrist back in place and I spent the next few weeks with one arm in a full cast above my elbow and the other in a splint. I remember it being slightly annoying to have to get sponge bathes and to have people at school help me do my work.

After that I broke each arm one other time before I was 11. None of the breaks were a fun experience that I want to relive, so I can't even imagine what life would be like if I were born with the disease Osteogenesis Imperfecta (OI).

OI is a disease that causes your bones to be brittle and prone to breaking. The simple act of coughing or sneezing could fracture a rib. There is nothing about OI that is fun.

One of the people I look up to the most in the personal development world, Sean Stephenson, was born with OI. He was literally born with every bone in his body broken. Doctors gave him 24 hours to live. Miraculously, Sean lived long past the 24 hours. By the time Sean was 18 he had fractured his bones over 200 times. Seriously. 200 times.

As a child, fitting in with everyone else was not something that Sean ever did well, so he loved Halloween. It was the one day of the year when everyone looked different therefore Sean fit right in.

On Halloween morning 1988, when he was nine years old Sean broke yet another bone--his leg after catching it on a door--leaving him unable to participate in his favorite holiday and keeping him immobile until it healed. In agony, Sean screamed, "Why Me, What did I ever do to deserve this?"

As Sean screamed this question, his very wise mother asked him a question that changed his life, "Is this going to be a gift or a burden in your life?"

day 23: *bones*

Sean had a choice to express gratitude or disgust over the bones he's been given. Thankfully, he made the decision to view the fragility of his bones as a gift that would help him "help those who were fragile on the inside in their spirit" and "to teach others how to love their life amidst their pain," as he has said to the millions of people he has impacted.

As a teenager Sean met Peak Performance Coach Tony Robbins who shared with Sean that his bones were breaking because they were acidic and encouraged Sean to follow a plant-based diet, removing foods that cause acidity in the body, such as sugar and processed foods. Sean changed his diet and did not beak another bone until a freak accident several years later, when his pet dog pulled his wheelchair and threw him out of it.

Sean continues to make the world a better place by serving as a speaker, author, and therapeutic coach with the motto "Riding the World of Insecurity" (check out more of his story in his book "Get off your 'But': How to End Self-Sabotage and Stand Up for Yourself"). If there were anyone who could claim the right to be insecure, it would be a 3-foot tall guy with arms that cannot reach over his head who is confined to a wheelchair, yet he doesn't.

Along with his beautiful wife, Mindie Kniss, Sean has touched the hearts of millions of people including the Dali Lama, Sir Richard Branson, President Bill Clinton and Jimmy Kimmel. Sean's smile is infectious and his wisdom is beyond his years.

Regarding the inner-conversations we have with ourselves, Sean said,

"When we sell ourselves the lie that we're not 'enough' or we're flawed or broken in some way, we short-circuit all our hopes and dreams. This kind of self-talk defeats us before we even begin, and makes it virtually impossible for us to look in the mirror and see the whole human being who's really there."

Whether or not you have all 206 bones functioning perfectly or not, the fact that you can hold this book is reason to be grateful. Our bones work hard for us each day with little appreciation.

day 23: *bones*

When we put unhealthy food in our bodies, we wear our bones out faster as it causes them to become acidic and become weak. Our bones are constantly worn down and remade literally to the point where every seven years we essentially have new bones.

Imagine how strong your bones could be in seven years if you feed your body nourishing veggies and let yourself know how loved you are each day?

Today, I invite you to experience the day with a joyful curiosity of how incredible your skeletal structure is. As you express gratitude throughout the day, allow yourself to sit in the quietness of gratitude and feel in your bones exactly how fortunate you are to be you, because there truly is no one else in the world like you!

day 23: *bones*

it's time to get naked!

morning

1. Set a timer for 1 minute.

Look at yourself naked in the mirror, scanning your body from head to toe, standing in awe of the brilliance that is your body.

2. As you look at yourself naked in the mirror state today's PVS --

I love my bones. My strong, healthy bones support me through every stage of my life.

3. Close your eyes and imagine what your bones look like under your skin. Think about all of the ways they have supported you already and thank them for their hard work.

4. Write down 5 things you are or could be grateful for about your bones.

♥ _____

♥ _____

♥ _____

♥ _____

♥ _____

day 23: *bones*

during the day

Whenever you stand today, thank your bones for their strength and power.

evening

1. At the end of the day review your 5 reasons to be grateful for your bones. Say, "Thank you, thank you, thank you" to your bones and feel the gratitude for the amazingness that is your bones.

2. Before you go to bed, say the PVS one more time and thank your bones for being uniquely yours.

Be thankful for what you have; you'll end up having more. If you concentrate on what you don't have, you will never, ever have enough.

Oprah Winfrey

day 23: *bones*

day 24: *powerful pancreas*

First, I eat healthy; it comes from the inside out. If you eat right, your skin, hair, nails will look good. The same if you have negative thoughts - they can give you a bad look, too; we reflect what we eat and think. We also taste and smell what we eat. Being happy and doing what I love really reflects.

Kate del Castillo

day 24: *pancreas*

positive vibration statement

My pancreas is amazing. I choose to experience love, joy, and happiness throughout the day.

day 24: *pancreas*

"Justin! My blood sugar is low, leave me alone or I will KILL you!!!"

This is a statement my younger brother heard almost daily when we were kids. Being the typical younger brother, he always thought it was funny to annoy me, especially when my blood sugar was low and would do everything in his power to push every button I had. To me, it was as if he had a death wish.

On day 15 I told you the story of how I was diagnosed with low-blood sugar after passing out on our back porch when my sister was giving me a perm. The only instructions I received from the doctor were to "not eat sugar," so I wouldn't become diabetic.

He didn't explain to me what I was doing to my body when I was eating sugar. He didn't explain the damage that I was doing to my pancreas and how that damage would impact every second of my life.

I'm guessing that unless you've had issues with your pancreas, you may not have given much thought to it before today.

Where is the pancreas and what does it do you ask?

Your pancreas is located in the upper part of your abdomen, behind your stomach, and is approximately 6 inches long. Some describe your pancreas as having a head, body, and tail.

The head is located near your liver and is connected to the first section of the small intestine. The tail runs under your stomach towards your spleen.

The pancreas is one of the few organs in the body that belongs in both the endocrine and exocrine systems.

Within the exocrine system, it aids in digestion as it releases digestive enzymes allowing the body to process food and to obtain the nutrition that's needed to function.

As part of the endocrine system it releases hormones (insulin and glucagon) into the blood after you eat, helping to control your blood

day 24: *pancreas*

sugar levels. Insulin is needed to lower our blood sugar levels while glucagon is needed to raise blood sugar levels.

Basically, the pancreas plays an essential role in converting the food we eat into fuel for our bodies' cells. This conversion of food impacts our hormones, which in turn control our emotions.

Additionally, when our pancreas becomes imbalanced we can experience conditions such as type-2 diabetes.

Type-2 diabetes is a direct result of dietary and lifestyle choices. Foods and drinks that are highly refined and full of sugar make the pancreas work so hard that it eventually stops creating insulin. Typically, people are first diagnosed as pre-diabetic (or hypoglycemic). Then, if they don't make shifts to their diet and lifestyle, they exhaust the pancreas' ability to produce the necessary hormones, and they become a type-2 diabetic requiring insulin injections or medication.

The good news is, all of this can be prevented or reversed. My dad was a type-2 diabetic on medication. Once we shifted his diet, he was able to go off his medication and he released 40 pounds in the process!

I have no doubt that if you are a woman reading this, you can think back to at least one time in your life when your blood sugar level was not optimum and you acted in a way that you knew was not "you." That reaction was because your hormones were out of whack and could possibly be that your pancreas, along with some of your other organs were not happy.

In many ways, the pancreas has the huge job of allowing us to be the beautiful, fun, playful, and happy women that we are. When it has all the things it needs to do its job it can work amazingly. When it doesn't....well, we all know who we become.

If you want to have a happy pancreas show it love by feeding it foods that are whole or as close to their whole form as possible. Reduce the amount of sugar you consume so that your pancreas doesn't have to work so hard. If you are going to have caffeine or alcohol, let it be just enough to satisfy your taste buds.

day 24: *pancreas*

Let your pancreas know how grateful you are for the job it does every day by releasing the right hormones and digestive enzymes you need to keep you from being "hangry" (that's hungry and angry together).

Your pancreas wants the best for you. As you go about through today, each time you are about to eat or drink something, ask your pancreas, "Will this make you happy?" Yes, it sounds cheesy, but you'll be surprised at how your body will speak to you and tell you what it needs--when it's given the opportunity to speak.

day 24: *pancreas*

it's time to get naked!

morning

1. Set a timer for 1 minute.

Look at yourself naked in the mirror, scanning your body from head to toe, standing in awe of the brilliance that is your body.

2. As you look at yourself naked in the mirror state today's PVS --

My pancreas is amazing. I choose to experience love, joy, and happiness throughout the day.

3. Focus your attention on your pancreas. Place your hand on the upper part of your belly and bottom of your rib cage over your pancreas. Take a deep breath in and think about everything your pancreas does to keep your hormones stable. As you inhale and exhale, thank it for all the work it does to keep you happy.

4. Write down 5 things you are or could be grateful for about your pancreas.

♥ _____

♥ _____

♥ _____

♥ _____

♥ _____

day 24: *pancreas*

during the day

Periodically today, thank your pancreas for all the work it does to help keep your emotions level.

evening

1. At the end of the day review your 5 reasons to be grateful for your pancreas. Say, "Thank you, thank you, thank you" to your pancreas and feel the gratitude for the amazingness that is your pancreas.

2. Before you go to bed, say the PVS one more time and thank your pancreas for working so hard to keep your hormones even.

It is impossible to feel grateful and depressed in the same moment.

Naomi Williams

day 24: *pancreas*

day 25: *happy, balanced kidneys*

There is nothing more rare, nor more beautiful, than a woman being unapologetically herself; comfortable in her perfect imperfection. To me, that is the true essence of beauty.

Steve Maraboli

day 25: *kidneys*

positive vibration statement

I love my kidneys. I only eat and drink what makes my body feel smart, sexy, and vibrant.

day 25: *kidneys*

According to Chinese medicine, kidneys are considered the organ connected to water and are in charge of storing our "essence." Our "essence" is defined as the foundation of the human body, influencing the abilities of reproduction, growth, and development.

Each day the kidneys work, without a break, to filter out approximately 50 gallons of blood through 140 miles of tubes and millions of filters to produce one to two quarts of urine a day. That's a huge job!

When our kidneys are functioning at 100% our physical vitality and mental clarity is abundant and our nurturing and protecting characteristics are strong. Doesn't that sounds like an amazing way to experience life?

On the contrary, if we have any imbalances in our kidneys and they are not functioning at 100% we may feel fearful, depressed, indecisive, isolated, confused, and lacking in courage. These emotions are the complete opposite of living a smart, sexy life full of vibrant energy.

In the spring of 2014 I experienced this first hand during a 9-day coach-training program. Knowing that I would be staying in a hotel with limited access to healthy foods, I literally brought a portable kitchen with me and made my own food each day.

Many of my colleagues teased me about the cooler I carried around with me until they were starving. Then, suddenly I was their best friend and they hoped I would share my food (I didn't. I'm admittedly selfish when it comes to sharing food).

Each day my cooler was filled with green smoothies, salads, hard-boiled organic, and other delicious treats, many of which were raw. I was definitely eating "clean." (Well, some would argue that eggs are not a clean food, other than that, everything I had was a fruit, veggie, or non-glutinous grain.)

By the third day of the training, I sounded like I had bronchitis, mucus was flowing out of my nose like a dam that had been breached, I could not stop crying, and I was having suicidal thoughts. For the rest of the

day 25: *kidneys*

training I seemed like someone who could not pull herself together emotionally.

None of it made sense to me. These were all of the symptoms I would get when I ate gluten or sugar but I hadn't had a drop of either. I felt as if my body was betraying me as my essence and vibrant energy was nowhere to be found. I was angry and I let my body know how angry I was with it!

Never one to want to just manage the symptoms, when I arrived home I took massive action to figure out the underlying cause of the symptoms. I ordered a food sensitivity test and headed to my local Chinese doctor of Traditional Chinese Medicine.

Both revealed a high sensitivity to eggs, bananas, and almonds (all of which I ate daily while at the training) and that my kidneys were imbalanced.

My Chinese doctor put me on an incredibly strict diet that consisted of a limited amount of "warming" foods (i.e., a small list of foods I could eat and they all had to be cooked or baked). I stopped eating eggs, bananas, and almonds, plus I gave a lot of love to my body by resting and only speaking positive things to it.

Within 3 days of making these changes all of my symptoms cleared and I was back to my happy, pleasant, mucus free self. It was as if my essence was free to shine because my kidneys were balanced again.

The intelligence that our bodies have is absolutely astounding. Sadly, Western culture trains us to not take the time to listen to its wisdom. We've been trained to listen to what everyone else tells us rather than listen to what our own bodies need.

As you've gone through the process of looking at yourself naked each day expressing gratitude for your unique body, my desire is that you will become more connected to it. As you become more connected to your body, you will be able to listen more to what it needs to find balance.

day 25: *kidneys*

As you go through today, think about the primary emotions in which you live. If you find that you may lean towards feelings of sadness, fear, indecisiveness, or confusion your kidneys may need some love.

If you have never experienced these feelings on a long-term basis, thank your kidneys for doing such a great job!

As you look at yourself naked today, I invite you to place your hands on your hips then slide them upwards until you can feel your ribs with your fingers. Your kidneys are at the back, under your thumbs. With your hands there say, "Thank you, Kidneys, I love you!"

Consciously think about your kidneys with each sip of water you take today. Thank them for how they filter your blood so that you can stay vibrant. Thank them for regulating your body's fluid levels so that you can live in health.

Give your kidneys a lot of love today, so they can love you back!

day 25: *kidneys*

it's time to get naked!

morning

1. Set a timer for 1 minute.

Look at yourself naked in the mirror, scanning your body from head to toe, standing in awe of the brilliance that is your body.

2. As you look at yourself naked in the mirror state today's PVS --

I love my kidneys. I only eat and drink what makes my body feel smart, sexy, and vibrant.

3. Focus your attention on your kidneys. Place one hand on each side of your spine beneath your ribs, where your kidneys are. Take a deep breath in, think about everything your kidneys do to filter your blood, and let them know how much you appreciate the work they do for you.

4. Write down 5 things you are or could be grateful for about your kidneys.

♥ _____

♥ _____

♥ _____

♥ _____

♥ _____

day 25: *kidneys*

during the day

Every time you eat or have a drink today, thank your kidneys for keeping your healthy.

evening

1. At the end of the day review your 5 reasons to be grateful for your kidneys. Say, "Thank you, thank you, thank you" to your kidneys and feel the gratitude for the amazingness of your kidneys.

2. Before you go to bed, say the PVS one more time and thank your kidneys for working so hard to keep your blood filtered and vibrant.

Gratitude and attitude are not challenges; they are choices.

Robert Braathe

day 25: *kidneys*

day 26: *brilliant ovaries*

Turns out ovaries work just as good as balls when you're in the driver's seat.

Reece Butler

day 26: *ovaries*

positive vibration statement

I love my ovaries. I own my amazing power as a woman. I lovingly accept each stage and process my ovaries experience.

day 26: *ovaries*

As women, we are all very well aware of the emotional roller coaster that we ride on a daily basis. One minute we are elated and excited about everything in our lives, the next minute everything seems hopeless.

I know that what I am about to say next may sound crazy, but that roller coaster of emotions is what makes us so incredible. We are a storm of emotion—that's part of being feminine. It's much of what makes us so alluring to the masculine man.

Yet, as women, most of us would love it if we weren't so "emotional." And, if that were true, we'd be men.

This storm of emotions begins to brew as we head into puberty as our body produces hormones that stimulate the ovaries to wake up our eggs each of which has the potential, by coming into contact with sperm, to become an embryo (the fact that we have, inside our bodies, the ability to create another human life is beyond unbelievable to me!).

The hormones that we have the privilege of having from puberty to menopause let our bodies know that it is now the phase of life when we can reproduce. And every month, as our body goes through its cycle, we are reminded of just how "feminine" we are.

I will admit, there was a time in my life when I didn't think or believe that being a woman was so amazing. From my teens through my twenties, once a month my body literally felt as if an alien had invaded it. It seemed to do everything it could to get all of my insides to be on the outside.

For 24-48 hours I would experience severe cramps, vomiting, and diarrhea —all at the same time. The amount of school, work, and events I missed due to my "femininity" was ridiculous. There was nothing I could imagine to be grateful for during those hours spent curled up in a ball, on the toilet, or with my head in a trashcan.

Fortunately for me (and all those who were around me during my "time of month"), I did eventually learn how to care for my body so

day 26: *ovaries*

that it didn't experience such distress during my period (more on that later).

Fascinatingly, each month our ovaries produce two different hormones—estrogen, and progesterone—and they know exactly when to release each of them.

We need the estrogen to thicken the lining of the uterus in case there is an embryo produced that month. Progesterone is needed to prepare the lining of the uterus to support embryo implantation and the establishment of pregnancy.

If there is a pregnancy, the ovary continues to produce progesterone until the placenta is formed and can take over, typically during the 12th week of pregnancy.

If there is no pregnancy, the ovary knows to stop producing progesterone, causing the uterus to shed it's lining, which is when we get our periods. Thank you very much, Mother Nature!

When you consider the fact that your ovaries know exactly which hormone to produce at exactly the right time, it is astounding! There's no need for you to set a reminder on your phone to tell your ovaries to send in more estrogen. No need to set a reminder to stop producing progesterone. Your ovaries just do it automatically. Mother nature is quite brilliant!

Sadly, just as I experienced in my teens and twenties, I know that many women experience the same pain each month and curse their ovaries rather than praising their brilliance.

What I didn't realize all those years of horrific periods was that my body was not only shedding the lining of my uterus each month, but it was also literally shedding everything else it didn't need that I had put inside of it.

For me, that was the build up of all of the things that caused toxicity in my body—dairy, gluten, and sugar. Once I eliminated them from my diet, my cramps, vomiting, and diarrhea disappeared. Granted, I still

day 26: *ovaries*

have slight discomfort, but it's more like a rating of .05 on a scale of 1-10 compared to before when it was a 50 on the same scale.

Each month when I was cursing my ovaries, I didn't really need to be cursing anything. I just needed to make some changes in my life to better support my body.

That has been true for every woman that I've coached as well. When we switch from cursing our nature to expressing gratitude for the brilliance that is our body, then we begin to connect with what it is our body truly needs to operate at its highest level.

As I said, for me, that was eliminating gluten, dairy, and sugar. It wasn't always easy and there was certainly a transition time of several months before all of the pain went away, but it has been well worth it.

Could there be anything that's standing in the way of your body operating at its highest level?

Take a moment to put your hands on your lower stomach between your belly button and your pubic bone. Close your eyes and take a deep breath. As you inhale and exhale slowly, ask your ovaries if there is anything they need to be able to work as brilliantly as they can.

If you don't feel like you are getting an answer, spend the day sending your ovaries love and gratitude. Then, do it again tonight before you go to bed. You may be surprised at the message you receive. Trust the message and give your ovaries what they need.

Allow all of the feelings that come with changing your diet and lifestyle to be noticed, acknowledged, and thanked. With each tear, say "thank you," with each joyful minute say "thank you," and allow yourself to be curious about the messages you receive. You may be surprised at how you are able to create ovaries that work brilliantly, which in turn, create a smarter, sexier, happier you!

day 26: *ovaries*

it's time to get naked!

morning

1. Set a timer for 1 minute.

Look at yourself naked in the mirror, scanning your body from head to toe, standing in awe of the brilliance that is your body.

2. As you look at yourself naked in the mirror state today's PVS --

I love my ovaries. I own my amazing power as a woman. I lovingly accept each stage and process my ovaries experience.

3. Focus your attention on your ovaries. Place your hands on your lower abdomen, right about where your hipbone is. Breathe deeply allowing your abdomen to extend and as you exhale bring your belly button back to your spine. Thank your ovaries for all of the work they've done for you up to this point in your life and for how they will continue to work for you each day.

4. Write down 5 things you are or could be grateful for about your ovaries.

♥

♥

♥

♥

♥

day 26: *ovaries*

during the day

At least a half a dozen times today, thank your ovaries for the work they do or have done for you (set an alarm on your phone to remind you).

evening

1. At the end of the day review your 5 reasons to be grateful for your ovaries. Say, "Thank you, thank you, thank you" to your ovaries and feel the gratitude for the amazingness of your ovaries.

2. Before you go to bed, say the PVS one more time and thank your ovaries for being uniquely yours.

Gratitude is more of a compliment to yourself than someone else.

Raheel Farooq

day 26: *ovaries*

day 27: *vagina - a place of pleasure*

> *Why do people say 'grow some balls?' Balls are very weak and sensitive! If you really wanna get tough, grow a vagina! Those things take a pounding!*
>
> Betty White

day 27: *vagina*

positive vibration statement

I love my vagina. I am grateful for my sexuality and all that it allows me to experience in life.

day 27: *vagina*

In the first go-around of writing this book, it never crossed my mind to include the "lady parts."

One of my clients was going through a rough version of *28 days naked* and she said that she was surprised I didn't include the vagina or ovaries as they are so important to who we are as woman. Duh! Of course, they are, I thought.

Then, I realized I had a fear of writing about being grateful for our vaginas. My mind flashed to the unforgettable "vagina scene" in the 1991 movie *Fried Green Tomatoes*. You know the one where Evelyn goes to a woman's empowerment meeting and runs away horrified when the woman in charge announces that they are going to start off with everyone looking at their vagina in a mirror?

I was afraid that anyone reading this would have the same reaction that Evelyn did, and just stop reading. Then I realized that this part of our bodies truly does deserve our attention and gratitude.

For many women the vagina can be a very scary part of the body. There is an interesting YouTube video that shows grown woman looking at their vagina for the first time (search YouTube for "women see their vagina for the first time" to see the full video).

When asked why they hadn't seen their vagina, their responses ran the gamut.

"My stomach is covering it and I don't have eyes on the bottom of my stomach"

"I wanted to be a nun."

"The first guy that went down there told me it was hideous and disgusting."

"I was raped and just pushed it out of my mind."

The women were then escorted (individually) into the "Vagina Booth" and given a hand-mirror to look at their vagina for the first time. What

day 27: *vagina*

was most amazing about their reactions was their lack of shock at their lady parts. Even the former aspiring nun said, "Awww" when she looked at herself.

They all realized that their vaginas were not what they had believed them to be.

If you grew up in a religious environment you may believe that looking at your vagina, let alone touching it is a sin, making the feelings you have about your vagina "bad."

Or you may have grown up in a family that celebrated your sexuality and you've had a healthy relationship with your vagina for as long as you can remember.

The first time I looked at my vagina with a mirror I felt so much guilt and shame because I had grown up in an environment where anything sexual was "bad." The irony is that there is nothing "sexual" about looking at a part of your body. It's no different than looking at your elbow or your knee. It's only sexual and "dirty" if you choose to make it such.

We all have the ability to associate either pain or pleasure to our vaginas. If we've had experiences that were painful, we tend to associate continual pain.

Like the woman who believed the guy who said her vagina was "hideous and disgusting," we can believe anything we want about any part of our body, even our vaginas. And, just as she realized when she looked at it, our beliefs are not always reality.

Today, I invite you to "get intimate" with your vagina. As you look at yourself naked, look at your vagina (if you want to bust out a hand held mirror to look at it, more power to you!)

Think about how it was created to be so many things, one of which is to be a place of pleasure. Think about how it is the entrance to a beautiful part of our bodies that has the ability to create life. Think about all of the orgasmic moments you've experienced because of

day 27: vagina

your vagina, whether this was with a partner or by yourself. Thank it for all of the moments of releasing built up sexual tension that allowed you to collapse in the best possible way.

If you are reading this and you start to feel sad because you cannot have children, think about how your vagina is the place that has the ability to give you the greatest pleasure—an orgasm (there really is nothing like a good orgasm).

If you've never had an orgasm, becoming more in-touch with your body through daily gratitude is a great place to start to allow yourself the freedom to just "be." After all, relaxing and being comfortable in one's own skin is the first step to experiencing a mind-blowing orgasm.

As you go through your day, each time you find yourself taking your underwear down, whether it is to use the bathroom, to change clothes, or to take a bath or shower, thank your vagina for everything it's done for you.

If you are feeling a little saucy today, give it some pleasure—you and your vagina will be grateful you did!

day 27: *vagina*

it's time to get naked!

morning

1. Set a timer for 1 minute.

Look at yourself naked in the mirror, scanning your body from head to toe, standing in awe of the brilliance that is your body.

2. As you look at yourself naked in the mirror state today's PVS --

I love my vagina. I am grateful for my sexuality and all that it allows me to experience in life.

3. Focus your attention on your vagina. If you are feeling adventurous, get a hand held mirror to see what you can't see with a regular mirror. Thank your vagina for being a place of pleasure and life.

4. Write down 5 things you are or could be grateful for about your vagina.

♥ _____

♥ _____

♥ _____

♥ _____

♥ _____

day 27: *vagina*

during the day

At least 6 times today, thank your vagina for its strength and power. (Set an alarm on your phone to remind you.)

evening

1. At the end of the day review your 5 reasons to be grateful for your vagina. Say, "Thank you, thank you, thank you" to your vagina and feel the gratitude for the amazingness that is your vagina.

2. Before you go to bed, say the PVS one more time and thank your vagina for being uniquely yours. And, if you have the opportunity, maybe allow your vagina (and the rest of you) to experience some pleasure before going to sleep!

Whoever has gratitude (for health) will be given more, and he or she will have an abundance. Whoever does not have gratitude (for health), even what he or she has will be taken from him or her.

Italian Proverb

day 27: *vagina*

day 28: *the breath of life*

Improper breathing is a common cause of ill health. If I had to limit my advice on healthier living to just one tip, it would be simply to learn how to breathe correctly. There is no single more powerful—or more simple—daily practice to further your health and well being than breath work.

Andrew Weil, M.D.

day 28: *lungs*

positive vibration statement

My lungs are amazing. As I breathe in deeply, I fully receive all great things life offers me.

day 28: *lungs*

Breathing and respiration are essential to everything we do. We can go 3 weeks without food, 3 days without water but only 3 minutes without breathing. To say that our lungs are a vital part of our well-being is quite an understatement.

I had never given much thought to my lungs and their health until I came down with walking phenomena in my early thirties. I was making massive changes to my diet and was experiencing what many experience when they work to become healthy—the Herxheimer Reaction.

The Herxheimer Reaction is an immune system reaction to the toxins being released when you start to kill off the pathogens by adding in nutrient dense foods and other healing modalities. To put it simply, it is the body's reaction when it is detoxifying and releasing toxins. It seems counter-intuitive that one would get sick while attempting to improve one's health, but it is actually healthy as it is our bodies' way of creating room for health and is a sign that healing is taking place.

I wanted you to know this so if you experience the Herxheimer Reaction you can now smile knowing that you are on your way to health and you can just say "thank you" to your body for releasing the toxins and creating room for health to come in!

I had just learned about the Herxheimer Reaction before I contracted walking pneumonia. Up to that point in my life, my lungs had seemed to be relatively weak. Any kind of cardio exercise made me feel like I was dying (okay, maybe that's a little bit of an exaggeration but it certainly felt like death to me), so it was natural that my lungs would experience a sort of "healing crisis" as I made changes to my diet. With each cough and contraction of my chest I expressed gratitude that I was moving closer to my outcome—to have vibrant energy—and I specifically thanked my lungs for doing their job so well.

Our lungs' primary job is to process the oxygen we inhale. Barring a birth defect, we all have two lungs, one on each side of our chest, together weighing 2.9 pounds. Prior to researching for this book, I didn't know that the left lung is lighter and smaller than the right lung, it has only two lobes compared to the right lungs' 3 lobes, and it is

day 28: *lungs*

structurally different than the right lung due to it's placement by the heart (isn't our design amazing?).

Scientists estimate that the total internal surface of an adult lung, if it could be stretched our and laid flat, is equal to the total area of one side of a tennis court, which is crazy when you think about how compact they are inside of our bodies.

Every day our lungs breathe in and out about 2,100 to 2,400 gallons of air. The brain and lungs work directly together since the brain is capable of sensing oxygen concentration in the air. Depending on how much oxygen you need, your brain increases or decreases your respiration rates.

Our ability to breathe is both an involuntary and voluntary act. Each second we unconsciously breath in and out. Yet, we can also, at any given second, decide to consciously change how we are breathing. We can decide to breath fast or slow, deep or shallow, and we can choose to stop breathing altogether (until our unconscious steps in and reminds us that life is worth living).

When we choose to consciously breath, we trigger our parasympathetic nervous system to counter our sympathetic nervous system's "fight or flight" response to daily stress.

We literally have the ability to increase our mental and physical health just by changing our breathing. Study after study reveals that when we spend daily time controlling our breathing (aka meditation) we literally change how we feel, how we behave, what we attract into our lives, and how we respond to the curveballs life throws us. This is why we always hear the advice "just breathe" when we are feeling stressed.

As you are reading this, take a deep breath in through your nose while counting to four. Now, hold it for a count of seven and then release it to the count of eight. Then repeat. You can do this until you feel calm and peaceful.

day 28: *lungs*

This is an exercise I learned from Dr. Andrew Weil. It works wonders whenever there is any kind of internal conflict brewing such as stress, anxiety, trouble falling asleep, or having a food craving.

If you haven't yet experienced the benefits of conscious breathing I invite you to take some time today to do just that. Some quick ways to start are by doing the exercise above right now. You can also search "guided meditation" on YouTube for a plethora of choices.

One of my favorite resources for clients starting meditation is an app called "Headspace." It is simple and easy to understand, and the narrator's voice is lovely (every client I've recommended it to has loved it).

With each inhalation and exhalation you take today, as much as possible, say in your head, "Thank you. I'm so grateful." Some people find that setting a timer to go off at the top of every hour to remind them to do a short breathing exercise is helpful. Other people like to put post-it notes in places where they will see them often. Do what works best for you.

When you lay your head on your pillow tonight, look back over your day and observe the differences you experienced as you spent the entire day in gratitude. It's amazing what a difference those two little words can make!

day 28: *lungs*

it's time to get naked!

morning

1. Set a timer for 1 minute.

Look at yourself naked in the mirror, scanning your body from head to toe, standing in awe of the brilliance that is your body.

2. As you look at yourself naked in the mirror state today's PVS --

My lungs are amazing. As I breathe in deeply, I fully receive all great things life offers me.

3. Focus your attention on your lungs. With each inhalation and exhalation allow your lungs to be filled with air and gratitude saying, "Thank you, thank you, thank you!"

4. Write down 5 things you are or could be grateful for about your lungs.

♥ _____

♥ _____

♥ _____

♥ _____

♥ _____

day 28: *lungs*

during the day

At the top of each hour, take a few deep breaths and feel gratitude for all breath and life.

evening

1. At the end of the day review your 5 reasons to be grateful for your lungs. Say, "Thank you, thank you, thank you" to your lungs and feel the gratitude for the amazingness of your lungs.

2. Before you go to bed, say the PVS one more time and thank your lungs for giving you the breath of life needed each day.

Gratitude can transform common days into thanksgivings, turn routine jobs into joy, and change ordinary opportunities into blessings.

William Arthur Ward

day 28: *lungs*

a smarter, sexier, happier you

Everything that is in your life is because you have created it. You may not be able to control the circumstances of what has happened to you, but you are able to control how you respond to those circumstances.

As I mentioned before, when I first heard this, I thought the person who said it was absolutely crazy, rude, and unsympathetic. Now, I realize that it was one of the kindest, most loving, and most sympathetic things she could have ever said to me.

I didn't need someone to join me in the pity party of my life. I needed someone to tell me the truth about my life. And the truth was, I was so focused on everything I didn't have that I was making myself miserable. No one else was doing it to me; it was all my choice.

Once we switch from focusing on what we don't have to what we do have, magic happens.

In life, attitude is everything. One of my favorite quotes about this comes from pastor and author Charles R. Swindoll:

> The longer I live, the more I realize the impact of attitude on life. Attitude, to me, is more important than facts. It is more important than the past, than education, than money, than circumstances, than failures, than successes, than what other people think or say or do. It is more important than appearance, giftedness or skill. It will make or break a company…a church…a home.
>
> The remarkable thing is we have a choice every day regarding the attitude we will embrace for that day. We cannot change our past…we cannot change the fact that people will act in a certain way. We cannot change the inevitable. The only thing we can do is play on the one string we have, and that is our

attitude. I am convinced that life is 10% what happens to me and 90% how I react to it. And so it is with you...we are in charge of our attitudes.

Through this practice of *28 days naked* you have laid the foundation for an incredible relationship with your body. As your love for yourself increases and improve, other areas of your life will also increase and improve. You will begin to notice how other people respond to you differently, how you are more open to opportunities that come your way, how you smile more, and how you "don't sweat the small stuff." People can't help but be more attracted to you as you grow in your gratitude.

I invite you to continue this practice beyond these 28 days. Every 3 months, go through this practice again to reinforce the foundation you've built. In between doing this practice, there are three other things I invite you to do:

- ♥ Every day, whether it's the first thing in the morning or the last thing at night, write down at least three things you are grateful for.

- ♥ Set a "gratitude alarm" on your phone during the day to remind you to give thanks.

- ♥ When you find yourself wanting to say something negative about your body, replace it with thanks.

There are also so many other great books on gratitude that can help deepen your practice. Go to Amazon and type in the word "gratitude" — over 24,000 books come up. See which one (or ones) speak to you, place an order, read, and continue to learn and grow.

The more genuine gratitude you express for your body, the more it will be open to healing any ailments, the more you will see it's beauty, and the more you will feel smarter, sexier, and happier.

When self-loathing, self-doubt, fear, frustration, stress, depression, unhappiness, or anger is the problem, gratitude is always the answer.

You have the power within you to have the life you want through those 2 simple words "thank you!" Literally, health and happiness are just two words away—two words that can never be overused and never run out. Use them liberally and watch your world transform!

Thank you for joining me on this 28-day journey. My wish and desire is that you truly do feel smarter, sexier, and happier than you did 28 days ago!

> *In daily life, we must see that it is not happiness that makes us grateful, but gratefulness that makes us happy.*
>
> Brother David Steindi-Rast

about the author

As a former mental health counselor, Heather struggled with depression and health issues until her early 30s. Never considering food and lifestyle to be the culprit of her issues, Heather blamed everything else for feeling terrible—until she discovered that her health issues (emotional and physical) were created by what she ate and the thoughts she choose to focus on. Heather then headed back to school to The Institute for Integrative Nutrition to add Health Coach to her resume.

After using her new knowledge to cure herself of hypoglycemia, low-grade depression, and menstrual issues, Heather discovered that she enjoyed cooking and decided to attend The Natural Gourmet Institute to become a chef.

Within 2 years of graduating culinary school, Heather co-founded the country's first bakery free of gluten, dairy, eggs, soy, corn, and refined sugar. She and her bakery have been featured on The Food Network's *Cupcake Wars* and the Cooking Channel's *Food(ography)* and *Unique Sweets*.

In 2012, Heather sold her shares of the bakery. She then added Master NLP Practitioner and Master Weight Loss Coach to her resume. And, in 2014, she became a coach for Peak Performance Coach Tony Robbins.

Heather combines her coaching skills with a form of energy work, developed by Dr. Bradley Nelson called The Emotion Code and Body Code, to help hundreds of men and woman get past the hurdles that are keeping them stuck, such as anxiety, limiting beliefs, shame, excess weight, and food addictions so that they can have the life of their dreams.

Heather also wrote *Smart, Sexy Sweets, Decadent Desserts That Happen To Be Free of Gluten, Dairy, Eggs, Soy, Corn, Nuts and Refined Sugar*, available on Amazon.

In addition to one-on-one coaching, Heather provides group coaching programs, and speaks to groups on health, wellness, personality and behavior motivators and how to create a life you love. She also provides one-on-one cooking classes as well as demonstration cooking classes.

When Heather isn't coaching, you can find her either with friends or flying through the air as an aerialist.

For information on her schedule and availability for coaching or to have Heather come speak to your company or group, email: heather@heathere.com or visit www.heathere.com.

Made in the USA
Columbia, SC
18 June 2017

CONTENTS

Foreword / 4
Poetry / 5
Fiction / 23
Articles / 36
Plays / 55
Local History / 76
Copyright and Contracts / 88
Computers, Yes or No? / 93
Bibliography / 95

FOREWORD

This book is designed to help you become a better, more efficient writer. Hopefully it will not only lead to increased sales but to greater joy in your chosen field of writing. Writing is communication between one person and another at a high level of understanding and in a permanent form. Whether you are just starting out or are already a published writer in some field, it is well to keep in mind these words of William Faulkner, "It is the writer's privilege to help man endure by lifting his heart".

POETRY

Poetry is literature written in meter or in verse form. It is perhaps the most personal of all types of literature. Some people have referred to it as the "shorthand" of literature. Certainly it is usually more restricted in length than any other form.

You write poetry because you are sensitive to life and to your experiences. You write poetry because you want to record your observations and the conclusions that you have made in your private voyage of discovery.

1. WHAT ARE THE VARIOUS TYPES OF POETRY?

A good book on literary terms will give you the fullest definitions of the various types of poetry. A textbook or handbook on poetry will give you all the poetic ramifications of the forms that can be used. Here, however, are some of the most popular forms with short definitions.

Ballad	A narrative poem, usually short and comparatively simple.
Blank Verse	Unrhymed iambic pentameter.*
Free Verse	Poetry that is not dependent upon regular meter or a set length of line. Usually un-rhymed, it is closely allied to natural speech patterns.
Haiku	From the Japanese. A three-line poem with 17 syllables, 5 in the first line, 7 in the second and 5 in the last.
Light Verse	Usually meant to entertain, often humorous. Limericks are one form of light verse.
Lyric	Poetry that expresses personal feelings and emotional responses. Usually not too long a poem.
Ode	A lyric poem which is more serious and considerably longer than the usual lyric poem.
Sonnet	A poem of 14 lines and a set rhyme scheme. It is usually written in iambic pentameter. There are several different kinds of sonnets.

*Iambic pentameter. A foot is the basic measurement of rhythm in poetry. The iamb is a foot of verse which has an unstressed syllable followed by a stressed syllable. A pentamenter is a line of five feet, as shown in the following example from Shakespeare:

"Shall I compare thee to a summer's day?"

2. HOW OR WHERE DO I GET IDEAS FOR POEMS?

You are surrounded by ideas! The trick is to train yourself to be receptive to those ideas. Unlike some fields of writing, you do not need to travel to faraway places or have any special knowledge other than a knowledge of words and their meanings.

What can you write about? Start with yourself and your perceptions of the world around you and your responses to other people and to situations. You have a whole universe in yourself. You know that you wouldn't want to write poetry if you were not a sensitive individual. Exploit that sensitivity in your poems. Don't be afraid to be personal.

Write about your surroundings. There is poetry there whether you live in a crowded city, suburbia, a small town or in the country.

Write poems about what you see, what you feel and what you dream about.

Be alert for ideas for poems. They will not come at a set time but at any time and not always, I admit, the most convenient time. Make a note of the ideas, the random line that comes into your head or the word that suggests a poem so that you can work on your poem when you have time.

Your poetry should be a kind of diary of your life.

3. AREN'T SOME SUBJECTS MORE SUITABLE FOR POETRY THAN OTHERS?

No, just as there aren't words that are set aside for poetry, so there are no special poetic subjects. If you will look in any good anthology of poetry or look at a collection of a poet's works, you will see the diversity of subjects that are covered.

What you are probably thinking of is that there are some subjects that all poets seem to write about at one time or another in their careers. Love is, of course, the best known of these. Nearly all poets have written some love poetry and even people who don't claim to be poets will write a love poem or two when under the influence of Eros!

A look at poetry will also show that current events are a frequent choice of both contemporary poets and poets of the past. This is in the tradition of the ancient balladeer or wandering minstrel.

You can write a poem about any subject. You will probably not choose to do so. You might, however, try your hand at a variety of subjects just to see what you can do. This is a good exercise in developing your poetic skill and in enlarging your vocabulary.

There is also a side bonus — writing a poem about a subject will give you a new insight into it. You may find your ideas changed by what you discover.

4. WHAT KIND OF POETRY SHOULD I WRITE?

I hope that you will write all kinds of poetry. You will, of course, find in time certain forms or a certain style that becomes the truest expression of your poetry. This then, will be known as your "style."

The subjects of your poems will at times dictate the kind of poems you write. Above all, don't be afraid to experiment!

The poetry you write should be in direct response to your experiences and feelings. You cannot go far wrong if you stick to what seems most natural for you as a poet.

5. DOES POETRY HAVE TO RHYME?

No, a poem does not have to rhyme, but it may. Whether or not you use rhyme will depend upon the form you have chosen and the subject matter.

If you use rhyme, be careful not to fall into writing doggerel which rhymes but lacks the true music of poetry.

You can have fun working rhyme into your poetry by using interior rhyme instead of having rhyme at the end of the line. You can follow traditional rhyme patterns or develop your own.

Rhyme can be good discipline, just as writing in prescribed forms can be exercises with which you develop your poetic skills.

The best advice I can give you is neither to scorn rhyme nor to become dependent upon it.

6. HOW LONG SHOULD A POEM BE?

A poem should be just as long as is needed to adequately cover the subject matter of the poem. Some subjects are more suited to haiku than to an epic and vice versa.

The pitfall in length is that many poets, even experienced ones, may write too many lines. This is "overkill" in poetry. Once you have developed your idea, you don't need to keep repeating it!

In marketing poems, as a rule, short poems (those under 20 lines) have a better chance of publication than long poems. This is due to economics rather than taste, for the cost of publication is such that not many magazines feel they can afford to devote their space to long poems. They would rather publish 20 short poems by twenty different poets than a twenty-page poem by one poet.

A beginning poet should probably stick to short poems, for it takes skill and practice to sustain the idea in a long poem. But, if you have a subject that demands the longer form and you feel up to it, write the poem. There are some magazines that have no length limits and there are also occasional contests for the long narrative poem.

Remember that in essence, it is the subject that dictates the form and the length.

7. AREN'T SOME WORDS MORE POETIC THAN OTHERS?

No. All the words in your dictionary are potentially poetic words. Poetry is not a separate language. It is a special way of using words. Modern poetry, in particular, uses all kinds of words.

Now, not all words are successfully used in a poem, but that is because those words don't belong in that particular poem. They might work very well in another poem.

In the past, and particularly in Elizabethan times, there were certain words which were used by poets just as some stock characters were used by dramatists. Words like *o'er*, *'tis*, *ere* and *oft* appear over and over again. Today we are not bound by these cliches. Poetry is no longer a language apart. The poetic beauty of a word becomes apparent when it is properly used in a poem.

8. WHY IS A KNOWLEDGE OF WORDS AND THEIR MEANINGS SO IMPORTANT TO A POET?

If you were a painter, you would expect to learn all that you could about pigments, brushes and canvas. If you were a composer, you would expect to be able to read and write music and to know about musical instruments and the human voice. As a poet, you have to know about words. They are your raw materials.

You can write a poem using very few words, true, but they have to be the right words. The wrong word is like a false note or a jarring, out-of-place color in an otherwise flawless composition.

Your dictionary is an invaluable tool. It will give you all of the meanings of a word, not just the one that you are perhaps accustomed to. Studying the meanings will help you to pick the right word to express yourself in your poem.

9. HOW MUCH OF A VOCABULARY SHOULD I USE IN MY POETRY?

Don't be afraid of words! Your dictionary is your storehouse of potential words for your poems. Use words that you are comfortable with and whose meanings are clear to you. Don't use words that are obscure or long just to be using words. The vocabulary of the poem should be consistent with the idea of the poem. One poem may call for very simple words while another will require more complex words. It is your privilege and responsibility as the poet to select the right words for the poem.

Start your writing with words that you know, but keep increasing your vocabulary. "Collect" words and make them a part of your vocabulary. Learn the various meanings and nuances of words. In this way you will know when a word is used appropriately and when it would be out of place.

10. WHY IS IT IMPORTANT TO USE CONTEMPORARY LANGUAGE IN MY POETRY?

You should use contemporary language because you are a contemporary poet writing for a contemporary audience. You want to be understood by your readers. While you will often write about situations and emotions that are ageless, you want to express these feelings in words and phrases that will be alive to today's readers.

11. HOW CAN I DEVELOP AN "EAR" FOR POETRY?

While poetry is written and usually read, it is really meant to be spoken and heard. Poetry is a highly musical art. A true poem, no matter what its form is, should have the same kind of rhythm that a musical composition has.

You have to develop an "ear" for poetry just as you would for music. To do this you must not just write and see your poems, you have to hear them.

When you are writing, or if that is not convenient, after you have finished a poem, read it aloud, not once but many times. Your ears will catch nuances that your eyes would pass over. Most people tend to read intellectually, but they listen emotionally. A good poem combines intellectualism and emotionalism. You can be sure that your poem does that if you use both your eyes and your ears in writing.

And, when you read your poem aloud, listen to what you are saying. Listen for sense, rhythm, and evenness of flow. A word or phrase out of place or an awkward construction will show up very quickly when you hear it spoken.

The first poets were in existence before words were written down. They were the first historians, the first to keep alive the tribal traditions. They did it through the medium of the spoken word. Their audience was limited to those who could hear them. You can reach a much wider audience, but the same principles of rhythm and interesting content are still in operation today in order for you to hold your readers' attention.

12. HOW WILL A TAPE RECORDER HELP ME WITH MY POETRY?

There are two ways in which a tape recorder can help you. It can help you write better poetry and it can help you to be able to read your poetry aloud and do it justice.

We have talked about developing an ear for poetry. A tape recorder can help you do that. You may either use it when you are working on a poem or during the process of revision. For example, suppose that there is a particular line that you are working on and you have thought of a variety of words that seem to convey the idea of the poem. Sit down with your tape recorder and record these various lines. This will work best if you also record the lines that precede and follow so that the line you are working on is not taken out of context.

Now play back the tape. Listen carefully. You will probably play it back several times. Your ears will tell you what line or combination of lines sounds the best.

Let us suppose that you have finished your poem. You are very satisfied with it. You have done all that you can do. That's fine, but why not test it against your ear? Do it either now or in a day or so. Tape the poem and listen. If it sounds exactly as you want it to, then that poem is ready to send out. Many times, however, you will find that you want to change a word or two.

Your tape recorder lets you hear your poems as another person will hear them. It helps you step back and look at your poems more objectively.

All poets are asked at one time or another to read their poems aloud for an audience. It may be for the radio, a local club, a group of friends, a television program or a writing club. You don't want to do your poems a disservice by reading them badly.

Your tape recorder will enable you to hear how you sound to others. Record some poems and then listen as if you were in the audience. Check off these points:
1. Is my speed right? (Some poets read so fast that all sense of poetry is lost, while others read so slowly that they lose their audience completely.)
2. Am I talking distinctly? (The mumbled phrase or word destroys the poem for the listeners.)

3. Is my tone varied enough? (Many people, when they read poetry aloud, develop a monotonous or singsong tone. Remember, you are reading words which have rhythm. You want to convey that to your audience.)
4. Am I talking loudly enough and maintaining my volume through the entire poem? (Remember that you will often have to read without a microphone. Don't shout but speak loudly enough so that you can be heard by everybody, not just the people in the first two rows. And don't drop your voice at the last line or two. I have heard many good poems ruined by the last lines not being clearly audible.)
5. Am I too "choppy" in my delivery? (The poem should read as a continuous whole, not as a series of isolated words, phrases or lines.)
6. Have I paid attention to the punctuation in the poem? (Punctuation in poems helps you to know where to pause, to breathe and when, in its absence, you should glide into the next phrase or line.)

All of the points given above can be taken care of by using your tape recorder as a guide. Not only will you be better at reading your poems aloud, but you will also find that it will help you in writing them in the first place.

13. SHOULD I READ THE WORKS OF OTHER POETS?

Yes, you should read the works of both modern poets and poets of the past. You will especially want to know what kind of poetry is being written and published today. After all, these poets are your contemporaries.

You should also be well acquainted with the poets of the past years. Read both the best-known poets and then look up some of the lesser poets, also. Don't forget that the Elizabethan period was one of the most fertile periods in English literature.

When you read poetry, remember that you want to read in two ways. First, read it for pure enjoyment and then, second, read it in an analytical way.

Dissect the poems to see their form; their rhyme scheme, if any; their use of imagery and all other pertinent facts related to the craft of writing poetry. Now this doesn't mean that you are going to like all of the poems that you read or agree with the way in which they have been written. It will help, however, to give you a deeper background in poetry than the casual reader has.

One of the best ways of getting acquainted with the poetry of any period is to start with a good anthology of that period. Modern anthologies are also a way of keeping up with today's poets.

Reading, studying and analyzing the poems of other poets does not mean that you are going to imitate them in your own work. The understanding that you gain through reading can be applied to your own poems to make them uniquely yours.

14. SHOULD I WRITE MY POEMS IN LONGHAND OR ON THE TYPEWRITER?

Whether you write poems out by hand or use a typewriter is mainly a matter of personal preference. Choose the method that is most comfortable for you. Some poets find that the mechanics of a typewriter seem to defeat their creativity, but there are others who feel that there is no barrier with a typewriter.

Your choice will also depend upon your surroundings and your situation. If you do not have ready access to a typewriter, then you will probably have to write in longhand.

This is what I have found to be most practical. I write my poems first in longhand, usually in my poetry notebook. Later, I transfer them to the typewriter, making further revisions at that time.

Seeing the poem typed gives you the opportunity to see what it will look like when it is published. It is easier to judge length of lines when the poem is typed. Any misspellings will show up more readily in the typed version. It is also easier to see whether or not the proper punctuation has been used.

One thing to remember about writing your poem in longhand — be sure and write legibly. It is very frustrating to write a great poem one day and then not be able to read it the next day!

15. WHAT IS THE VALUE OF A POETRY NOTEBOOK?

A poetry notebook is one of your most valuable tools. It is one of your literary assets.

Select a notebook that is most suited to your personal needs and habits. You may want one that fits in a purse or pocket. You may prefer a large, loose-leaf notebook.

What are you going to put in your notebook? You will want to put anything pertaining to poems that you are working on or poems that you hope to write some day. It is also a good place to record any technical information about poetry that you want to keep or remember.

A poem rarely comes to you in its complete, final form. If you write it in your notebook as you work on it, you will always know where it is. Later, when it gets to the right stage, you will be ready to sit down at your typewriter and work from your notebook.

Many times only a portion of a poem will be finished. You may start a poem in August but not finish it until October! You may take even longer and want to add to or change a poem over a period of weeks or months. Your notebook then becomes the ideal place in which to record all of these changes. When the time comes to write your poem in its final form, you have these preliminary words to work with.

Sometimes a single phrase or even a word will so take your fancy that you feel sure that there is a poem somewhere that will have to be written incorporating that phrase or that word. In the meantime, record it in your notebook. You won't forget that way. It's very frustrating and discouraging to try and recall some word or line after the immediacy of the moment has passed.

And there is another function that a poetry notebook fills — it will show you your own progression in terms of poetic skill. The more you work on your poetry, the greater use you will make of those words, lines and ideas that you have tucked away for the future.

By the way, be sure and keep your poetry notebook handy at night. You'd be surprised how many poems or ideas for poems will come to you after you have relaxed and gotten ready for bed. I always keep my notebook on my bedside table.

16. HOW DO I KNOW WHEN A POEM IS REALLY FINISHED?

Through experience, you will learn this, but sometimes even the most professional poets are troubled by the problem of ending poems.

One of the most common errors is to go on too long. This destroys the impact of the imagery of the poem and bores the readers.

When you first write your poem, don't worry about whether or not it is finished. Write what you have to say and take as many (or as few) lines as you seem to think necessary at the time. Later, during the revision period, you will want to examine the ending of the poem.

Have you overstated your case? Don't run your idea into the ground. Have you tried to tack a few lines of explanation or a moral on the end of your poem? This was popular in past centuries but it is not done now.

Does your ending relate to your beginning in the poem? A common pitfall for many poets is to cram too many ideas in one poem. Their beginning lines sometimes have little or no connection with their ending lines. You may have two poems in one.

17. HOW MUCH TIME SHOULD I SPEND ON REVISION?

You should spend as much time as is necessary to produce a poem that is as satisfactory as possible to you, its creator. I deliberately said "as satisfactory as possible," for no true creator is ever really satisfied. He (or she) feels instinctively that he could still make improvements had he time and knowledge enough to do so.

Usually when a poem is first written, there is that marvelous feeling of accomplishment, a feeling of euphoria that is almost overwhelming. The act of creation is the most satisfying of all the things that men and women do. The words of your new poem seem to sing and you sing inside yourself.

That's fine, but now put the poem aside for a period of time — even a few hours will help, but a day or two is better.

When you next look at your poem, the joy of final creation will not be blinding you to any of its flaws or to any possible changes. Now read the poem critically, almost as if it were not your own.

This is when you can use your tape recorder to good advantage.

Test each word, each phrase, each line; check punctuation and the way the poem holds together as a whole. Keep doing this until you feel that you have done the best that you can at this time. When you are satisfied, then it is time to send the poem out into the world in search of a publisher.

When rejected poems come back, take a fresh look at them for possible revisions. Since you are growing all the time as a person and a poet and your experiences are continually increasing, you may be able to add some new value to that rejected poem.

Revision is an art in itself. It demands patience, knowledge and a perceptive eye and ear.

Don't make a trap for yourself by insisting that each poem you write is instantly perfect and each word too precious to change. The willingness and the ability to revise are hallmarks of the true professional.

18. CAN I REALLY SELL MY POEMS?

Yes — sometimes. If you will look at your market lists, you will see that there are some newspapers and magazines, that pay for poems. You won't be able to make a living selling your poetry, but if you are a good poet and persistent at sending out, you should be able to at least make enough money to pay for your supplies and postage.

You will find that many of the poetry or literary journals do not pay except in copies. Some of the journals offer yearly prizes or a free year's subscription.

Trade, fraternal and religious periodicals will usually pay for poems. Again, your market lists will tell you which ones pay and how much they pay.

There is a limited commercial market for poetry. Usually a poet is more interested in publication than in payment.

19. SHOULD I HAVE AN AGENT FOR MY POETRY?

No, because poetry is such a specialized market, an agent can not do anything more for you than you yourself can do. And, since agents take a fee, usually 10% for each sale, and the money from poetry sales is negligible, it would scarcely be worth your while or the time of the agent. That is why very few agents handle poetry.

20. SHOULD I SEND OUT POEMS REGULARLY?

Yes. In fact, I recommend that you set aside a specific period each week to send out your poetry. If you work, you may want to set aside some time on the weekend or one evening. If you are at home, you should set aside some time weekly during a morning or afternoon.

Having the habit of sending out your poems regularly means that you will always have poems out in circulation. Keep reminding yourself that your chances of publication are zero unless you get those poems out to editors.

21. WHERE DO I GET INFORMATION ON MARKETS FOR POETRY?

There are a number of very good professional sources of market news. There are two magazines that are published monthly. Both of these periodicals contain information about poetry markets as well as having special poetry market lists during the year. These two are:

The Writer,
8 Arlington Street
Boston, Massachusetts 02116

Writer's Digest
9933 Alliance Road
Cincinnati, Ohio 45242

Both of these magazines are invaluable aids in selecting poetry markets. If possible, subscribe to them; otherwise consult them at your local public library or buy copies at the newsstand.

There are also some books which have poetry market lists. Investing in these is mainly a matter of personal preference and economics. You may want to go to the library and use them there since some of them are fairly expensive. However, if you are doing other kinds of writing as well as writing poetry, you will probably want to have them in your personal library. These are: *Writer's Market, Writer's Yearbook, The Writer's Handbook.*

You will also want to note markets that you come across in your reading. Some of these may be newspapers and magazines published in your area.

Always be alert to various possibilities of publishing poetry. Just as a keen angler is always on the lookout for news of good fishing streams, so you must be on the watch for good poetry markets.

22. SHOULD I TRY TO GET A SAMPLE COPY OF A MAGAZINE BEFORE I SUBMIT POEMS?

This is simply a matter of personal preference. By consulting the market lists, you can get a fairly good idea of what a particular magazine or newspaper is looking for in poetry. However, if you feel that you would like more information, do get a copy of one of the issues.

Some magazines furnish sample copies to writers. They will usually indicate this in their market listing. Becuase of the increasing costs of publication, other magazines feel that they can not supply a free copy but will send one issue for their usual price or at cost. When you do not know what a magazine's policy is, drop them a postcard inquiring about single issues and if there is a charge.

Your local public library may be a subscriber to various poetry magazines. You should make it a habit to be familiar with their holdings in this field and to visit the library regularly to examine their poetry magazines. If you live in a college town where the college library is open to townspeople, this is another excellent source for examining magazines that publish poetry.

Since you, yourself, are a poet, I assume that you will, if you can, subscribe to one or more poetry or literary magazines. These you can consider as kinds of textbooks for you to study. Seeing what is being published will help you evaluate your own work.

Although I have been talking about poetry and literary magazines, don't forget that poetry is also published in other places. Look for the poetry in the newpapers you get or go to the library and look at their papers. Some trade magazines, house journals and many general magazines also publish poetry. Your market listings will tell you what newspapers and magazines publish poetry.

Remember, in studying these sample copies, you are not going to try and imitate what has already been published there. What you are doing is making a survey to see what types of poetry are being published in these magazines. For example, you will find that some periodicals want only nature poems, others will have length specifications, while still others will be interested in experimental verse only. You can also tell by studying these magazines and newspapers whether or not they are interested in publishing poetry by only well-known writers or whether their market is open to all poets.

23. DO I HAVE TO SUBSCRIBE TO POETRY MAGAZINES TO GET THEM TO PUBLISH MY POETRY?

The poetry magazine that requires you to be a subscriber to have your poems published is an exception. And, except in the very smallest magazines, the functions of the circulation and editorial departments are usually so separated that there is no knowledge of who, among those sending in poems, are subscribers and who are not. Being a subscriber to the average poetry magazine does not guarantee you an acceptance; it does give you some knowledge of how that magazine operates and what kind of poems it publishes.

There are some fraternal magazines, religious or professional periodicals that may expect you to be members of their organizations, but this is quite understandable since they are not generally open to the public.

Beware of the anthology that requires you to purchase one or more copies in order to be included. The compilers of most anthologies will send you a free copy after the book is out or, if they pay you for the use of your poem, you can purchase a copy from your bookstore.

While it is true that you may never get much money for your poems, don't be pressured into paying someone to publish them. If you are going to spend money, publish your own book.

24. HOW DO I GET POEMS READY TO SEND OUT?

You will find it helpful if you always have all the things in one place that you need in preparing your poems for submission.

1. Typewriter
2. White typing paper ($8^1/_2 \times 11$)
3. No. 10 business envelopes
4. No. 11 business envelopes
5. Stamps
6. File cards
8. Market lists

Type one poem to a page, double-spaced. Type your name, address, city, state and zip code in the upper left corner. Single-space this information.

Send from one to three poems to each magazine. Three is best since it gives the editors a good sampling of your work and a chance to make some choice.

Type your own name and address on the No. 10 envelope, put a stamp on and insert it with your poems in the No. 11 envelope. Your return address and the name of the magazine or newpaper should be on the No. 11 envelope. In sending abroad, be sure to add U.S.A. after your address and write the name of the country to which you are sending your poems in large letters after the periodical address. Do not use United States postage on your return letter for foreign markets.

Record the poems on your file cards.

Mail promptly and while these poems are gone, keep working on new ones.

It is a good idea to have a regular time each week which you set aside for sending out poems. All finished poems should be out circulating in the marketplace until they find a home!

25. SHOULD I WRITE A NOTE OR LETTER TO THE EDITOR TO GO WITH MY SUBMISSIONS?

No, this is not necessary. Your poems will be accepted for themselves, not because of you or where you have previously published. Most editors are too busy in any case to read lengthy letters of explanation. It is the poems they want to read. After your poem is accepted, they will want to know more about you and what other things you have done, had published or are planning.

26. HOW DO I MAIL MY POEMS?

Once you have prepared your manuscript you are ready to mail. Send your poetry first class. It is inexpensive and guarantees a more prompt delivery.
Before sealing up your envelope, run through this brief checklist:
    1. Have I enclosed my self-addressed, stamped envelope?
    2. Have I recorded which poems I am sending to what place?
    3. Do I have the complete address, including zip code, on the envelope?
    4. Is my return address on the envelope?

If you are sending poems to a foreign market, you can not use United States postage on your return envelopes. At the Post Office you can buy International Postal Reply Coupons in the amount needed for return postage. The postal officials can tell you the amount needed to send and return your poems. It is best to send poems by air mail to foreign countries. Be sure to enclose the International Postal Reply Coupon with your poems.

27. WHAT KIND OF RECORDS SHOULD I KEEP?

It is important to keep accurate records of the poems that you send out and the places to which you send them. You will also want a record of what happens to the poems and if you sell them, you will want to record what payment you received. Later, when a poem is published, you will want to record the name of the magazine and the number and date of the issue in which your poem appeared.
I suggest using file cards for your records. Use either the familiar 3 x 5 cards or the larger 5 x 8 cards. Cards with lines will be easier to keep up and will look neater. Have a file box for the cards, either metal or heavy cardboard with alphabet guide cards.
You are really going to have five different files, although you will probably keep them in the same file box. They are:
    1. Markets
    2. Poems In
    3. Poems Out
    4. Poems Accepted
    5. Poems Published

In the first file list your most often used markets with all information pertinent to that market. For example:

> *Desert Voices*
> P.O. Box 1322
> Santa Fe, N.M. 87504-1322
> J.E. Ellis, editor
> Pays $5 per poem + 2 copies

In the second through fifth sections are the cards which tell you at a glance where your poems are or what has happened to them. You will need a file card for each finished poem. That card should include the title of the poem and may, if you wish, also include the date that you wrote the poem.

Use the symbols "R" and "A" to denote type of action taken by the periodical. R = Rejection and A = Acceptance. We hope that there are lots of A's in your file!

This is what your card might look like:

> Sea Night Song   Oct. 1982
> 10-12-83   *New Yorker*   R
> 11-15-83   *Aspects of Art*   A

When your poem has been accepted, the file card for that poem should go in the section headed ACCEPTED. After the poem has been published, you should bring your card up-to-date and then file it in the section headed PUBLISHED. Your card for "Sea Night Song" might look like this at that time:

> Sea Night Song   Oct. 1982
> 10-12-83   *New Yorker*   R
> 11-15-83   *Aspects of Art*   A
>   Published in the March
>   1984 issue of *Aspects of*
>   *Art*, Vol. 5, No. 3.
>   Rec. $5 and 2 free copies

Always keep your cards up-to-date so that you have at your fingertips a complete "case history" of each poem. If, after a poem is published, it is also reprinted in an anthology, that, too, should be entered on your cards.

By keeping adequate file records, you will not make the mistake of sending the same poems to the periodicals which have already rejected them. Also, you will be able to easily compile bibliographical information when you need to know where and when you have published. An up-to-date list is invaluable when preparing a book of poetry for publication.

To easily identify those cards which refer to accepted and published poems, I suggest that you put a small colored dot on the top of those cards. You can get packages of the signal dots at any stationery store.

Not only is the dot an identifying mark, but it will also give your ego a lift to put those dots on the cards!

28. **HOW LONG SHOULD I WAIT FOR AN EDITOR TO REPLY?**

As a poet, you are concerned with one, or possibly three, poems you have sent in to a magazine or paper. An editor is faced with hundreds of poems. This means that there has to be some lapse of time between submission and report and you always hope that it is a reasonable time.

The larger the magazine or newspaper, the quicker you will usually get a reply, simply because a large organization has more poeple to handle the incoming submissions. A small magazine has a small staff, often a volunteer staff. Naturally, it takes them longer to get through the mail.

A literary quarterly may have an Editorial Board that meets at regular but infrequent intervals to select poetry for publication and this means further delays. Some college or university magazines do not make any selections during the summer.

Market listings may tell you what to expect in length of time for a report. Personally, I always allow 6 or 8 weeks for a reply. After that, a card or brief letter of inquiry is not out of line. In most cases you will find that the editor has a good reason for delaying his reply to you.

Do, however, remember that with today's mail service, there may be delays before the poems ever reach the office of the magazine. Very rarely does a manuscript get lost in the mail, but it may be slower in reaching its destination than you expect.

Knowing the background and editorial set-up of a magazine will help you decide what is a reasonable time in which to expect a reply.

29. IF AN EDITOR WANTS ME TO CHANGE MY POEM, SHOULD I?

In most cases, I would say yes. Of course, to be valid, the change or changes should be ones that you agree with yourself. An editor can perform a useful function for you in pointing out the various possibilities of making your poem better or clearer. You, as the poet, are very close, sometimes too close, to what you have written to see it dispassionately. An editor looks at the poem without any personal attachments. He sees the poem as the readers will. And, while he sees the beauty and style, he is also very alert to any flaws. If he suggests a change of words or lines or even an omission of lines, you should try it the way he has suggested. If you don't agree, then you don't have to do it.

You may be sure that if an editor has taken the time to write some suggestions to you then he is interested in your poetry and in you as a poet.

30. MY POEM HAS BEEN REJECTED — SHOULD I GIVE UP?

Certainly not! Every professional writer can tell you stories about the poem that was rejected by twenty editors and was finally accepted by the twenty-first editor! Or the poem that no one seemed interested in until it won a prize. Yes, these things do happen.

But more than acceptance or rejection, publication or non-publication, the important fact is the writing. If you are a poet and you have faith in what you write, then you are not going to give up. This is not a short term project for you; this is a life-long love affair with words!

What should you do when your poem or poems are rejected? Of course you are disappointed, but don't allow yourself more than a few minutes of brooding, for you have work to do.

Also, don't be upset if you have received only a printed notice of rejection. The larger magazines and newspapers have so many submissions that they can't possibly write a personal note to all poets even when they would like to do so.

If an editor has written you a note, pay attention to it. An editor may have some valid suggestions for you, some words of encouragement for you or a request for you to send some other poems. Very often the poems you sent may not be just what the editor wants or needs, but he or his editorial board are impressed enough by your talent in poetry to want to see other examples of your work.

When your poems are returned, you need to get busy and get them ready to send out again. First, enter the rejection action on your file cards. Second, examine the returned poems. Do you think that any further revisions are called for? Read them over again just as an editor might. When you are satisfied with what you have, look at their physical condition. Do they need to be retyped? It takes only a few minutes to retype your poems and it is better to spend the time than to send out creased papers which look as if they have been making the rounds of editorial offices for some time.

Look up a new market for your rejected poems and send them out again. Do this as often as necessary. As long as you are convinced that those poems represent your best effort, keep them in circulation!

Remember that rejection by an editor does not necessarily imply lack of worth or lack of talent. It may simply mean that a magazine is overstocked or that it is the wrong market for your poems.

"Keep Trying" should be the motto above your desk.

31. MY POEM HAS BEEN ACCEPTED — NOW WHAT DO I DO

CONGRATULATIONS! Whether it is your first acceptance or your two-hundredth, there is no moment like that wonderful one when you read that note. You are going to see that poem in print or, as is the case with some newspapers, the poem has not only been accepted but already published and the tear sheets are in your hand.

After you have shared this with your family and friends, there are some practical things you have to do. Read the acceptance note carefully to see if the editor has asked you for any additional information. Many times editors will request some brief biographical details to use when they publish your poem. Send those out right away. They may be needed for the next issue. And, if they ask for "brief" details, be brief. Space for biographical information is usually limited to two or three lines for each contributor. List any other periodicals which have taken poems recently or the title of a book you have published or are going to have published in the near future. If you teach a class related to poetry, list that and the school in which you teach. If your work has appeared in any anthologies, give the titles. Keep the information short, pertinent and of most recent interest.

Now fill in your file card for that poem. See if the editor has said in what issue your poem will appear. Make a note of this and wait for your contributor's copy to be sent to you. If time passes and you do not get a copy, write and inquire. Copies are sometimes lost in the mail.

I recommend that near your desk or in some other handy and appropriate place, you put a bulletin board. Tack your acceptance letters up where you can see them. This is a great morale booster, especially on those days when there aren't any acceptance letters coming in. But knowing that you have had your poems accepted in the past should keep you going in the present.

Later, as you accumulate more and more acceptance letters, you will want to either file the old ones away under the name of the magazine or, if you prefer, keep a scrapbook.

Each acceptance should make you work just that much harder so that you can see an increasing number of your poems in print as time goes on.

32. WHAT ABOUT HAVING A BOOK OF POEMS PUBLISHED?

You might as well face facts about poetry in book form — it is very difficult to sell your collection of poetry to a big publisher. Poetry, unfortunately, does not sell well, and it is the exception rather than the rule that a book of poems pays its own way. Of course, there are some very well-known poets who become popular heroes and their books sell. The average poet, even if he has published extensively in magazines and newspapers, will often have a hard time convincing a publisher to invest in his book.

This is not meant to discourage you from trying, but only to prepare you for the kind of reponse you will probably get. At any rate, do not attempt to contact any publisher until you have had a large number of poems published in magazines, newspapers or taken for anthologies. That is your "track record" and when you contact a publisher you will want to list these places as well as the names of any prizes or awards you may have won for your poems.

Well, if book publication is so difficult, what are the alternatives? There are some, fortunately, so that you can see your book of poems in print after all, even if you aren't successful in getting a big publisher interested.

There are some smaller publishers that are especially interested in poetry. You can find their names and addresses by looking at the list of book publishers in your various market lists. One of the best lists can be found in the annual publication, *Writer's Market*.

Different from a vanity press is a good local printer or small press that will go in with you on your book. You pay for the printing costs and they pay for certain other costs — art work, advertisements, distribution costs, etc. — and then you split the profits, if there are any.

If there is a group of you who are interested in having your books published, you could form a small press cooperative. If there are some in the group who have the skills, you may do your own printing and binding, etc. If not, your group can work with a local printer.

Printing your own poetry book can be a lot of fun. Just keep in mind that you are not doing it to make money. You are doing it because you love poetry.

33. A BOOK OF MY POETRY IS GOING TO BE PUBLISHED. WHAT SHOULD I DO ABOUT THE POEMS THAT HAVE ALREADY BEEN PUBLISHED IN MAGAZINES, NEWSPAPERS OR OTHER BOOKS?

You can use your poems that have appeared elsewhere provided that you first get permission to do so from the original publishers. Your book publisher may get permission for you after you provide him with a list of where the poems have previously appeared or he may ask you to write for the permission. If you are publishing your own book, you will have to write the publishers.

Most editors and publishers are happy to give you the necessary permission. Their only requirement is that you give them credit in your book for having first printed your poem.

Make up a form permission letter to send. The body of this letter is the same for each publication. All you have to do is change the name and address of the recipient.

Here is a sample letter:

Marie Beaverton
132 Breckinridge Rd.
Austin, Texas 76012
December 10, 1983

The Sunstone Review
P.O. Box 2321
Santa Fe, New Mexico 87501

Dear Sirs:

A collection of my poetry entitled *Stars and Rockbound Earth* is being published this year. Included in the book are the following poems which originally appeared in *The Sunstone Review*:

"Web of Delight" Vol. 2, No. 4
"Time of Departure" Vol. 3, No. 2

I would like your permission to reprint these poems in the book. Credit will be given in the Acknowledgements.

Thank You.

Sincerely,

Marie Beaverton

When your permission letters are returned, put them in a file folder with the heading PERMISSION LETTERS if you are the publisher yourself. If a company is publishing your book, send the letters on to them. They will hold the letters in their files.

Once your book is out, be sure that either you or your publisher sends a copy to each one of the magazines or newspapers from whom you have received permission to reprint the poems. This is not only courteous but also, in many cases, the magazines will review your book.

34. I HAVEN'T BEEN ABLE TO WRITE ANY POEMS FOR A LONG TIME. DOES THIS MEAN THAT I AM THROUGH AS A POET?

No, every writer in every field of writing sometime or another experiences a "dry" period, but this doesn't mean the end.

You can sit around waiting for inspiration to strike you, but that's a little improbable as well as chancy. I suggest that you do something about this dry period yourself. If you were stranded on the desert, I am sure that you would start walking toward the nearest oasis. You wouldn't just sit there. Well, don't sit still and moan about your ruined career as a poet. There are things you can do.

Get out your poetry notebook. In it there should be some unfinished poems, some random words, phrases or ideas. Sit down and start working on one of these items. Don't expect miracles, but on the other hand, don't give up easily. Even if what you first write doesn't sound like good poetry, keep on trying.

Another way is to give yourself a topic and sit down and write a poem on that subject. This time don't be too concerned about poetic form or expression. What you are trying to do is to stimulate your creative ability. You can always go back and revise what you write.

Still another way is to take time to read poetry by some other poets. Suddenly you may find yourself overcome with your own ideas. At that time, put down your book and reach for your paper.

35. WHAT ABOUT WRITERS' CLUBS, CONFERENCES AND SIMILAR ORGANIZATIONS?

If your city has a writers' club and poets are included in its membership, I urge you to join. There is something very encouraging and stimulating about being able to talk "shop" with other poets.

Most states have a state Poetry Society. Sometimes the society will only have chapters in the larger cities. If you can attend their meetings, do so. Again, you will find that meeting with others of similar interests will prove to be a benefit.

If there is no poetry organization in your area and you know some other poets, why don't you get together and start your own club? In a club you can exchange information about markets, get helpful criticism about your work, and share the triumphs of publication.

Don't overlook the classes in writing given at your local college or adult education center.

36. DO YOU HAVE ANY FINAL WORDS OF ADVICE?

Yes, keep writing! Don't get discouraged and don't ever give up. Keep sending your poems out, keep studying poetry and put as much of yourself and as many of your experiences as you can into your poetry.

FICTION

The storyteller is a universal figure. As soon as men learned some methods of communicating with each other, there were stories to tell and share. It was the storytellers who, in earliest times, kept alive the history, myths and traditions of the people. Stories were told and retold, handed down from one generation to another. When writing developed, stories were written and preserved for all time; later, printing made stories accessible to everyone.

Fiction writers can look back to the legend of Scheherazade who saved her life by telling her husband stories in serial fashion for 1001 nights. Even today a good writer needs to emulate her example and make his or her fiction so exciting that the reader can't stop reading.

1. WHAT ARE THE VARIOUS KINDS OF FICTION?

When we talk of fiction we usually think of novels but there are also other forms to consider. The novella is a short novel. There are short stories and short, short stories which are usually one page in length. In addition, we can also divide fiction into such categories as historical, romance, mystery, science fiction, adventure and western. In the first case we are talking primarily about length, in the second we are classifying by genre, that is by subject.

2. WHAT TYPE OF FICTION SHOULD I WRITE?

The type of fiction you write will depend upon a) your interests, b) your experiences, c) your capacity for research. Obviously if you want to write science fiction you should have either a science background or access to information. If you want to write historical novels, you need to have background knowledge of the period that you select or the willingness to do the necessary research. A mystery writer who wants to use police in his or her fiction needs to have a knowledge of police procedures. Readers are quick to spot the fake or made-up, particularly if the novel is supposed to be realistic or authentic.

A good basic rule is to write about what you know and what interests you. Too often writers want to look for some more glamourous location or exotic subject than the one at hand. A well-written novel based on your location, your profession or your hobby may be your ticket to publication. If you do get to travel that's great, you have a wider pool of locations to draw upon. One writer I know has successfully combined his career as a travel guide with the writing of spy stories, all set in the places he visits.

Whether you choose to write novels or stories will depend upon your idea. Some ideas simply can not be expanded to the length required for a novel. Other ideas and characterizations can not be fully developed in a short story. You may have to experiment a bit to discover the proper length for your idea.

3. WHERE CAN I GET IDEAS FOR FICTION?

If you are a serious fiction writer, you will probably have more ideas than you can ever use. The first idea is the hardest, after that they proliferate like guppies! That is why you should keep either an idea notebook or an idea card file. Ideas do multiply but if you don't write them down, they have a way of vanishing.

You can get ideas from listening to people, listening to their stories, their life histories, their problems and concerns. Sometimes you get this directly by talking with them but very often it is by overhearing conversations. Make it a regular habit to observe people, their gestures, clothes, the way they sit, speak and move.

Read the newpaper regularly. It is filled with stories that may spark an idea in your mind. Clip out stories, items or pictures that particularly interest you.

Ideas only come if you are alert to them. Don't "wall" your writing self off from the rest of your life. If you are a writer, you are a writer all of the time even when you are working at some other job forty hours a week.

Read writers' magazines. You can often find an idea in an article or be stimulated by a note about current needs in the publishing field.

Read books. If you are a writer of historical fiction, you will want to have a regular program of reading in the period of history that you use.

Ideas literally surround you and you never know when you will find one that you can expand upon for a story or novel.

4. DO TRUE STORIES MAKE THE BEST FICTION?

Not necessarily. Remember the saying is "truth is stranger than fiction", not "truth is better than fiction". Most so-called true stories have to be changed to make good, saleable fiction. Use truth as your basis if you wish but artfully disguise it.

There is another problem with "true" stories. Authors who turn real life incidents into fiction without disguising either events or people have frequently found themselves engaged in libel suits. Don't take a chance! Your best friend may become your most agressive enemy if he or she thinks you have portrayed them in a novel or story, especially if they feel it is an unfavorable view.

As a writer it is your privilege to be able to rearrange facts to make better stories than reality provides. You can change events, add or subtract characteristics and alter lives in fiction.

5. IS THERE A HANDY FORMULA FOR FICTION WRITING?

Writing a story or a novel is not exactly like making a cake. You can devise an idea of what makes good fiction by studying the works of successful writers. However, for every rule that you discover, you will find writers who ignore it and achieve success by following their own ideas. You can work out your plot, allow so much for suspense, so much for romance, etc. but unless you make it a unique, individualized work, it will lack life and interest for readers.

A formula is only a guide line, a learning tool. Tell your story the best way you know, the way you would want to hear it.

6.   WHY SHOULD I MAKE AN OUTLINE?

An outline of your novel will help you to see where you are going and why. This is not to say that an outline must be followed slavishly for once you start writing, you will often find that characters change and events happen that mean new directions in action. Preparing an outline first though sweeps the cobwebs away. It is a plot summary that can also be used when you want to contact an agent or publisher.

As you write, keep your outline and character summaries before you. Some writers like to have them pinned or pasted up in front of their typewriters so that they are constantly in view.

You may also, espcially if your novel is long and involved, want outlines of the locations where incidents are taking place an a time schedule of events. When working over a long period of time, it is sometimes easy to forget where and when something took place.

SAMPLE OF PLOT OUTLINE OR SUMMARY

A SEASON OF WINTERS

Tim Dello, student of archaeology at Western State University, falls in love with Lucy Graves, daughter of Prof. Alban Graves of the Engineering School. Lucy is torn between her feelings for Tim and her desire for a career. An only child, she feels obligated to follow in her father's footsteps. After graduation, Tim goes to the Southwest to work on a prehistoric Indian site. While there he becomes acquainted with an Indian, Jim Lone Tree and his sister, Blue Star, both activists for Indian rights. They lead the opposition to the Dig but personally like Tim. Tim and Blue Star form a romantic attachment but finally cultural and political differences prove to be too much. They quarrel and break up. Greater trouble in the area develops when a power company decides to build a dam on the archaelogical site which is considered sacred ground by the Indians. One of the engineers on the project is Lucy Graves. Tim finds himself torn between his feelings for the two women and his...

SAMPLE OF LOCALE OUTLINE

Western State University — Chapters 1, 2, 4, 5
Boston — Chapter 3
Albuquerque — Chapters 6, 7
Desert — Chapters 8, 9, 10
New York — Chapter 11

SAMPLE OF TIME OUTLINE

Sept. - June 1980 = Chapters 1 - 5
July - Oct. 1980 = Chapters 6 - 7
Nov. - Dec, 1980 - Jan. - Nov. 1981 = Chapters 8 - 10
Dec. 1981 - Jan. 1982 = Chapter 11

7. WHAT IS A CHARACTER SUMMARY?

A character summary is a description of your fictional characters, their physical characteristics, mental attitudes, etc. This will help you not only to visualize them as "real" people but prevent you from becoming confused about them. For example, if in one place you refer to a character's *blue* eyes, you don't want to forget and later refer to his *brown* eyes. In working on a long novel over a period of time and with the natural interruption caused by your own life, you may forget details.

No character has to be fixed with unalterable characteristics for as the plot develops, you may decide to make changes. But keep your character summary up-to-date. You can keep it on sheets of paper or on cards.

CHARACTER SUMMARY CARDS

TIM DELLO: 22 at start of book. Tall (6'4") Graduate student of archaeology at Western State University, then archaelogist in the field (desert). Blond, blue eyes. Good sense of humor.

JIM LONE TREE: Indian (Navajo background) Medium build (6') Limps (Vietnam War injury) College graduate (economics major) Serious. Keen student of Indian history and traditions. Black hair. Wants to return to the "old ways".

8. WHAT IS A PLACE SUMMARY?

A place summary serves the same purpose as a character summary. It is to keep you reminded of the physical characteristics of places and how you have described them. It is also useful to indicate the ambience of places.

As with character summaries, these can be kept on cards or sheets of paper. You should be as familiar with the locations of your novel or story as you are with your own home town.

SAMPLE PLACE SUMMARIES

WESTERN STATE UNIVERSITY — Typical small midwestern university. About 13,000 students. old, Gothic-type stone buildings plus some new ones in brick.

CHET'S DINER — Favorite gathering place of students. Three blocks from the campus, on Main Street. Has booths, table & a counter. Limited menu, good coffee. Beer. Silver & gray decor.

9. WHAT PERCENTAGE OF MY FICTION SHOULD BE DIALOGUE AND WHAT PERCENTAGE DESCRIPTION?

There is no quick and easy formula. Your story line will determine how you mix dialogue and description. Dialogue should advance the story and be natural. Description is used to highlight and explain actions, settings and thoughts. The two must work together skillfully so that they become a single unity.

When using dialogue, be sure it is not stilted or stiff. Listen to the way people talk, listen to yourself talk. Dialogue should also be appropriate to the character of the person using it. Avoid the pitfall of using contemporary words or expressions in a novel or story which is set in the past. As with clothes, fashions in words change and readers will lose confidence in you as a writer if you are inaccurate in dialogue.

10. HOW MUCH RESEARCH DO I NEED TO DO?

Reserarch depends upon the subject you have chosen and your personal knowledge of that subject. An author who wants to set his fiction in Paris needs to be familiar with that city. The same applies if you are writing about a small town in Iowa or Indiana. You have to have first-hand information or you have to do extensive research by studying maps, photographs, histories and by talking to people who have been there. Whatever your setting — the theater, a meat packing plant, a library or a riverfront town, you need authenticity.

Research can be divided into two types: primary and secondary. Primary sources are peculiar to you. They can be your personal observations and experiences or they can be information gleaned from persons who have lived or worked in the setting you are using. Primary sources include interviews, unpublished letters, diaries and similar documents. Primary sources are particulary valuable when you are writing historical fiction which depends upon factual happenings.

Secondary sources are previously published works. Books, magazines and newspapers are common secondary sources. Research is usually a combination of primary and secondary sources.

Don't be so carried away by your story line that you neglect your research. There are always readers who are alert to any errors, false statements, anachronisms or wrong dates.

When deciding on a setting don't overlook your own past or present background and profession. What you know, where you have or do live can be fertile fields for your fiction.

11. I AM A POOR SPELLER AND "SHAKY" ON RULES OF GRAMMAR; WILL THAT BE A HANDICAP?

Yes. Editors have little patience with manuscripts that are filled with spelling errors and grammatical mistakes. If spelling is a problem, make it a rule to learn how to spell. You can get an English book suitable for children. This will also help you with grammar. Don't be afraid or embarrassed to go back to basics. Get a good dictionary and make it a practice to look words up whenever you feel at all unsure of the spelling. If your community has an adult education program there will probably be classes in English. You can also find helpful books at your public library. A fun way to learn more about words, how they are spelt and what they mean, is to do crossword puzzles.

12. HOW IMPORTANT ARE THE BEGINNINGS AND ENDINGS OF CHAPTERS?

Very important! If the beginning of your chapter is dull or lifeless, the reader may simply not bother going on. If your chapter ending is "flat", the reader has no incentive to turn the page and continue. A good test is to imagine the following scene. It is late at night, your reader picks up your book and begins to read. Will he be tempted to read on and on or will he lose interest and fall asleep? Or, will he turn on the late show on TV? Read your chapters as if you were that stranger. What would you do?

There's a lot of competition for the reader's attention in today's world. Can you compete?

13. HOW MUCH REWRITING SHOULD I DO?

Very few writers are so skillful that they can eliminate rewriting. The amount of rewriting you will have to do depends upon how well you write. Some experienced writers need only two drafts before going to final typing, others may write and rewrite five or six or more times before they are satisfied.

One method I have found useful is to write the first draft without worrying too much about spelling, grammar, etc. but simply concentrating on the story and its development. Some writers use a typewriter for that first draft, others prefer longhand and there are those who now use word processors. You should use the method that is the most natural and convenient for you. Nothing should get between you and your story at this point.

Your second draft should probably be typewritten and as you transcribe from your first draft, a natural process of editing should take place. It is now that you begin to notice and correct spelling errors, gramatical mistakes and obvious faults in the text. This second draft should be put aside for a few days and then read again in a critical fashion. This is when you should notice if there are loose ends, awkward spots in the dialogue and any lack of smooth transitions. Depending on what you find, you may need to do a third draft.

Continue to self-edit and rewrite until you are sure that you have done your best work. You may find it helpful to have someone else read it at this point. Ask this person to note any problems discovered in reading the story. Don't be insulted by what may be discovered. Be thankful you can make corrections and adjustments before sending your manuscript off for professional review by an agent or publisher.

14. DOES THERE HAVE TO BE SEX AND VIOLENCE TO SELL A WORK OF FICTION?

Yes and no. Yes in some markets but no in others. You have to decide which markets you want to pursue and what kind of writing you are going to be comfortable doing. If sex and violence bother you, don't use them. Look instead for markets (and there are a lot) that prefer fiction to be less graphic and more subtle. There is also a big market for fiction which is suitable for the religious marketplace.

15. SHOULD I SUBMIT MY ENTIRE NOVEL OR JUST PARTS OF IT TO A PUBLISHER?

Check your market information to see if the publisher has any specific requirements. Some publishers prefer to see the manuscript in its entirety, others want only a summary and sample chapters. If the complete manuscript is not wanted, send an outline or summary and sample chapters. This saves wear and tear on your manuscript. (It is also a saving on postage.) It is far easier to retype a few pages if they get wrinkled or dirty then to have to redo a whole manuscript.

If a publisher does not indicate any preference, send the summary and sample chapters. If they are interested, they will get in touch with you and ask to see the rest of the manuscript.

16. CAN I SEND TO MORE THAN ONE PUBLISHER AT A TIME?

Again this depends upon the publisher. In market lists you will find some publishers who state "simultaneous submissions ok". There are others who state they will not accept simultaneous submissions. If it is not mentioned in the listing, it is safer to assume they do not want simultaneous submissions.

17. CAN I SEND PHOTOCOPIES OF MY MANUSCRIPT?

With today's modern technology, most publishers are willing to accept photocopied submissions. To be sure, however, check the requirements in the market lists. Your copy should be crisp, clean and readable.

18. WHAT ABOUT COMPUTER PRINTOUTS OR DISK SUBMISSIONS?

A recent review of market lists showed that some publishers were willing to accept computer printouts but in other cases it stated such restrictions as "Disk submissions must be compatible with our equipment"; "prefer letter quality to dot matrix"; and "submissions must be printed on paper for our review process". As computers become more in use, particularly by writers, there will undoubtedly be some changes in requirements and more publishers will be willing to accept computer printouts and disks. Again the market lists should be checked for individual publisher preference.

19. WHAT KIND OF INFORMATION SHOULD I GIVE THE PUBLISHER ABOUT MYSELF?

Be brief and give only information that is pertinent to you as a writer and to your fiction. For example, if you have written a novel about Indians, it would be helpful for the publisher or editor to know that you spent ten years teaching in a Reservation school.

Always list other books you have had published, non-fiction as well as fiction. Quote from favorable reviews, particularly from major media. List any stories or articles you have had published and the names of the periodicals in which they have appeared. If you have had a large number published, make a selective list including the most recent and the most prestigious. Obviously the *New Yorker* carries more weight than the *Elm City Bugle*.

List any literary prizes you have received and related honors. Note any sales to foreign publishers, movies or television. If your work has appeared in anthologies, list their titles, date of publication and publishers.

Avoid vague, generalized statements such as "I've always wanted to write a book about daily life in Peru." or, "My friends think this is a good story and that it should be published."

A good rule of thumb is to put yourself in the place of the editor. Faced with your manuscript, what would you want to know about the author?

20. I WANT TO SEND A QUERY LETTER TO AN EDITOR BY NAME, HOW DO I FIND OUT HIS OR HER NAME?

Editors are listed in both *Writer's Market* and *Literary Market Place*. Use the latest issue (most libraries have copies), look up the publishing firm and its staff. In a large firm there will be several editors with differing responsibilities. Select the one suitable for your work. Don't send an adult novel to the children's book editor. Smaller firms may list only one or two names.

21. HOW DO I SEND OUT MY MATERIAL?

If you are sending a query letter, outline and sample chapters you can use a 9 × 12 mailing envelope. Include a second self-addressed stamped mailing envelope for the return of your material. Always be sure that the return envelope you include is the right size for the material you are sending.

If you are sending your complete manuscript, put the pages in a ream-size typing paper box. If you do not have a box, fasten your pages with a large metal clip or put them in an easy-to-open folder. When using or making a box, you may need to reinforce the corners of the box with tape. Include postage and a self-addressed mailing label.

While it is cheaper to mail manuscripts at the special manuscript rate, it takes much longer for them to arrive. First class mail while more expensive is worth the extra cost in the time it saves.

22. HOW LONG SHOULD I WAIT TO HEAR FROM AN EDITOR?

Six weeks is a reasonable time but some editors take more time, others less. You would certainly be justified in enquiring after six or eight weeks. Many publishers and magazines note their "turn around" time in their market listings. One publisher states "1 month on queries; 6 months on mss." so if you can't wait that long for a reply, you should try another publisher.

The time of the year will also have some effect on return response, especially in smaller places where there is not a large staff. Christmas time and August when people vacation usually mean a slower time in answering.

When you do not get a prompt reply, be realistic about what is happening for while it might be true that your manuscript is getting a careful examination it can be just as true that it has deadended on someone's desk.

A few publishers send a card or note saying that the manuscript has been received and indicate some length of time before you will receive a report.

23. WHAT ABOUT REGIONAL OR SMALL PUBLISHERS?

Don't overlook the regional or small publisher. There are many of them in all parts of the country. Some are connected with colleges, universities, societies or museums. The smaller houses operate to a large extent just as the larger houses but with less staff and often less capital outlay. They often are the ones who publish poetry and books on unusual subjects. The regional publisher specializes in non-fiction and fiction related to the area although they may also publish some non-regional material. If your book is regional, you may find it easier to sell to an area publisher.

On the plus side, smaller publishing houses give you very individual service. They are risking more in proportion than large houses when they select a book for publication so they are anxious to see it do well. They usually believe very strongly in what they are doing and see publishing as part contribution to history and literature and not just a commercial venture. At a smaller house, you will have an opportunity to know staff members who will be working on your book and you will be known to them as an individual, not just another author.

On the negative side, funds for publicity and advertising are often limited. Distribution may not be national and the sales force small or non-existent. Personal appearances, autograph parties, etc. will probably be limited to the local area. Smaller houses rarely give advances but most pay royalties. The market lists will give you that information.

The warm relationship you develop with a smaller publisher may outweigh the disadvantages.

24. I HAVE WRITTEN AND HAD PUBLISHED SEVERAL SHORT STORIES, CAN I PUBLISH THEM IN A BOOK?

Yes, if a publisher is interested in them. Submit two or three stories with brief comments about the others. Indicate which ones have been published, where and when. If there is a unifying theme that ties the stories together, note that also.

If a publisher wants them, you will have to get permission from the original publisher to reprint them. Your published book will list the earlier publications and their dates.

You can also combine published and previously unpublished stories in the same collection.

25. CAN I MARKET SECTIONS OF MY NOVEL?

Yes. Writers often sell sections of their unpublished novel to magazines. The section has to be "self-contained", that is have a logical beginning and end. It has to stand alone and not be dependent upon the larger work for interest and sense.

When you send out a section you should indicate that it is from a novel or a work in progress. If sections are published and later the novel is published, you must get permission from the original publisher and cite that credit in your book.

Having portions of your novel published in advance may help to sell the book to a publisher. In a sense it is also a form of market testing.

26. WHAT KIND OF RECORDS SHOULD I KEEP?

Even if you have only one novel that you are trying to market, you will want to keep a record of where and when it is sent. A card file, 5" × 8" works very well. On the card type the title of your novel or story and any other pertinent information such as the number of words. List where the material was sent, the date and if returned, the date and any important notations.

With these records, you will have a complete marketing history of your manuscript at your fingertips.

SEASONS OF WINTERS   75,000 words

Date	To	Action	Comments
10/12/83	Brooker Press	Ret. 10/30/83	Not accepting mss. at this time
11/3/83	Pilgrim Hall	Ret. 2/3/84	No comment
3/5/84	Spenser Press	Ret. 5/6/84	Suggest revisions
5/30/84	Spenser Press	Acc. 7/14/84	Contract to follow

The other records you need to keep are financial ones. You can use a ledger book or file cards. There are two basic records, one for money spent and one for money received. Such records are especially important when you are thinking of taking a tax deduction. Your accountant or tax person can give you precise advice on how to handle these financial matters. There are also certain records to be kept if you are using a portion of your home as your working office.

27. DO I NEED AN AGENT?

Undoubtedly an agent can do a better job of selling but it is not easy to get an agent until you already have some kind of track record in publishing.

Lists of agents can be found in *Literary Market Place* along with the type of material they handle. A recent publication *Literary Agents of North America* by Arthur Orrmont and Leonie Rosenstiel also has information that will help you pick an agent.

Some agents specify that they will not accept unsolicited manuscripts. Other state that they charge for reading manuscripts.

The best way is to write a query letter to an agent, describing your book and listing your qualifications, any previous publications and other pertinent facts. Don't forget to enclose a self-addressed stamped envelope.

Once you make that first book sale, you will probably want to contact an agent. An agent knows more about author-publisher negotiations, subsidiary rights and related items than the average author. Having a good agent can free you to concentrate on your writing.

28. DOES THE AGENT I SELECT HAVE TO LIVE IN NEW YORK?

No. More important than location is the kind of work the agent does. A good agent is aware of the trends in the publishing industry and has the knowledge of what can and should be done whether he/she is in New York City, Chicago or Des Moines. With today's modern and rapid systems of communication, the origin of the manuscript does not matter. As always what matters is the content of that manuscript and the professionalism of its presentation.

29. WHY SHOULD I READ PROFESSIONAL LITERATURE?

Writing like any other profession has certain professional journals and books. Reading these will help you to be informed about what is going on in the field of writing and publishing. You will be exposed to the writer's point of view as well as that of the editor and publisher. It is a way of knowing about marketing trends and needs, of changes in editorial policy, what books have been sold to the movies and a host of other useful facts. It is in these magazines that you can find names of editors, addresses of publishers and agents and what they need.

Two of the most prominent national magazines also have articles that offer practical help to writers. *Writer's Digest* and *The Writer* combine market news with "how-to" sections on all aspects of writing and marketing. If you write in the religious field there is *The Christian Writer*. *Publishers Weekly* has the latest information on publishing and the book trade.

Most public libraries carry the above titles and they can also be found at newsstands.

30. WILL BELONGING TO A WRITING GROUP HELP ME?

It will help you if your use it as a means of self-development and self-improvement. A writers club can be a useful forum for exchanging information about events and needs in the publishing field.

Many writers clubs schedule workshops and meetings with professional authors. They may also have critical sessions in which members' works are discussed. You can learn a lot by knowing how readers respond to your work.

Meeting and mixing with other writers can enlarge your horizons but only if this activity gives you pleasure. If you are a "loner" you may well prefer to get your information and help from books and magazines and not from other people.

If you do belong to a writers club don't fall into the trap of going to the meetings, talking about your proposed book and never really writing it.

Writing, itself, is a hard, lonely task and you may get needed inspiration and moral support meeting with others who share your same interests.

31. A PUBLISHER IS INTERSTED IN MY NOVEL BUT AN EDITOR SUGGESTS THAT I MAKE SOME CHANGES, SHOULD I AGREE TO DO THAT?

It is a rare author who is not advised to make changes by an editor. An editor brings to your work an unprejudiced, objective mind. He reads your manuscript for credibility and saleability as well as literary qualities. He knows what is involved in promoting and selling a book and whether or not your manuscript fits with established editorial policy.

Listen to the editor. That does not mean that you can't question the changes he or she suggests and certainly you are entitled to an explanation of why such changes are recommended.

Yes, you can refuse to change a single word or idea in your manuscript but in that case it is likely you will end up an unpublished writer.

32. WHAT IS AN ADVANCE?

An advance is prepublication payment on your royalties. Most large publishing firms give advances but the amount varies. The amount will depend upon who you are and what sales they anticipate. When you have had previous books published with good sales records, you can ask for larger advances. Small companies rarely pay advances.

33. WHAT ARE ROYALTIES?

Royalties are a percentage of the money received from the sales of your book. Most publishers give an accounting and pay royalties twice a year. The percentage you will receive is specified in your contract. Royalties range from 5% to 20% and may be paid on either the wholesale or retail price of the book. Some contracts provide for a sliding royalty scale of increased percentages as more books are sold. Some publishers pay different rates for paperback and hardback books.

34. SHOULD I EXPECT INSTANT SUCCESS WITH MY BOOK?

It is all right to expect it but at the same time you should be realistic. You may have written a "blockbuster" and will, as a result, achieve instant fame and wealth but the odds are against you. True, often enough first novels become overnight sensations, best sellers that are optioned for movies or television but these are the ones you hear about. In 1983 some 40,000 books were published and only a fraction of those made it into the big time; the others struggled along with average or slow sales. It is better to be happily surprised at what success you do achieve than to be disappointed at not being the number one book in the country.

Remind yourself that you may achieve greater heights with your next book or the book after that and in the meantime you are establishing a reputation as an author and gaining a faithful group of readers.

Only a select few appear on national televeision but there is much satisfaction in being on local or regional television and radio. And, even if the *New York Times* doesn't call you, a story about you in an area newspaper can boost your ego a lot.

35. I'VE TRIED AND TRIED BUT CAN'T GET ANYONE INTERESTED IN MY FICTION — WHAT SHOULD I DO?

First, ask yourself if fiction is your right field. If you have any doubts see if someone else such as a local writing teacher, editor, librarian or writer will look at some of your work. Stress that you want an honest evaluation.

Second, when you get this outside opinion or opinions if you want more than one, be prepared to accept them. If you're told that you just don't have a way with fiction, don't get angry or depressed. Say thank you and ask "why not?" and then listen to the reasons. One successful author I know couldn't get anywhere with his fiction when a reporter he knew suggested he try non-fiction. Recently his sixth non-fiction book was published. His problem was dialogue. No matter how hard he tried, he had no ear for how people talk. He killed his own stories everytime a character spoke. On the other hand if dialogue is your strongest point and description, your weakest, perhaps you should be writing plays.

Don't be afraid to experiment and try your ideas in different formats but if you are absolutely sure of yourself as a fiction writer, keep at it and don't give up.!

ARTICLES

One of the best opportunities for the free lance writer and for the beginning writer is in the field of articles. There are many more paying markets for non-fiction than there are for fiction, poetry or plays.

Article writing can be more easily and quickly learned than some of the other literary forms. You can develop a style and formula in writing articles that will make them salable.

This chapter is designed to help the beginning writer launch his or her article-writing career and succeed at it!

1. WHAT KIND OF ARTICLES SHOULD I WRITE?

There is no limit to the kind of articles that you write except for your ability to learn the facts or gather the figures needed for a specific article.

Your own special interests will probably determine to some extent what you write, but you do not have to confine yourself to those subjects. A professional writer will write on any subject that comes to his mind and for which he can find a market.

2. WHERE AND HOW DO I GET IDEAS FOR ARTICLES?

Ideas for articles are so plentiful that you will probably get more than you can ever use! Once you have trained yourself to think in terms of possible article usage, the ideas will come to you in all forms and shapes.

To start with, you, yourself, are one source of ideas. If you have a special skill, a hobby or a particular interest, the seeds for an article are there. Now look at your family, your friends and your acquaintances — do they have special skills, hobbies or unusual professions?

How about your town or area — does it have some unique historical, geographical or socioeconomic feature? Even if it has been written about before, look for an unusual and different slant.

Newspapers are a good source of ideas for articles. Read with that purpose in mind. Locally, you might read about an interesting personality, a new discovery or an item suitable for expansion into a full-length travel article. Don't overlook what is happening in your region for it has great potential.

A successful article writer has curiosity and he follows up leads when he comes across an item in a paper or magazine, even if it is only a few lines. He listens to people and to what they are interested in and what they ask about.

The "why" and "how" of any subject make good articles because they make good reading.

Don't say that there are no ideas where you are! I know one successful free-lance writer living in a small town who has written articles about such subjects as the town's struggle to establish adequate medical services, the reopening of a local mine, the story of a local handicapped woman who operated her own business and a score of other articles.

Ideas tend to mushroom and when you are working on one idea or doing research for an article, you will find that other ideas will come. One article often leads to two or three others.

Also, when looking for ideas, use your Million Dollar File (SEE No. 13). It is a storehouse of ideas just waiting to be used.

3.   SHOULD I HAVE A SPECIALTY?

Don't confine yourself to a specialty unless it is so large in scope that it offers limitless possibilities. If you are a home economist, you could specialize in articles dealing with various aspects of homemaking. If you are a psychologist or psychiatrist or minister, there are many markets for practical psychology and self-help articles.

If you have some special skill, hobby or profession, use it, but unless it offers continually expanding sales opportunities, don't confine your writing to that one specialty.

**4.   WHAT ARE THE BASIC STEPS
         IN WRITING AN ARTICLE?**

You start with an outline. This should be complete in the sense that it covers all of the points that you need to discuss in your article. If you are writing this article in reponse to an affirmative reply to a query letter, then you already have your outline prepared.

Tack this outline up where you can see it easily. This is your road map! On another sheet of paper list any special requirements the editor has made or that you know the magazine has. This sheet should also include the word limit that you have to keep in mind.

Next, do any research that you need for this article. It may be from files and books in your own office. You may have to spend some time at the library. You may have to consult with a specialist. You decide on what research is required by examining the outline. It will tell you what statistics you need and what facts. Very often an editor will ask that you put in certain facts and figures that he thinks will interest his readers. Note carefully what you need and gather up your material. For additional material on research and research methods, see Sections 10 and 11.

Once you have all of your material and notes, you are ready to sit down at your typewriter and write. By following the outline you will be able to progress rapidly from the beginning to the end.

After the first draft is finished, look it over for sentence construction, errors in spelling, logic and clarity. If possible, wait until the next day for this reading. After corrections are made, the final typing can be done. Always make a carbon at this time.

When finished, check for typographical errors, file your carbon, prepare your manuscript for mailing, enter the action taken on your record card, mail your article and wait for your check!

**5.   HOW CAN I FIND OUT IF THE IDEA I HAVE
         HAS ALREADY BEEN WRITTEN UP AND PUBLISHED?**

First, you will want to keep up yourself with what is being published in current issues — particularly in those periodicals for which you write regularly.

However, it is physically impossible to keep up with every magazine and newspaper. Fortunately, there are printed indexes which you can use to track down whether or not a similar article has been published in recent years. These indexes are available at the library.

The most useful one to you will be the *Readers' Guide to Periodical Literature.* In the front it lists all of the magazines which are indexed in it. there is also the *International Index To Periodicals* and it, too, lists what periodicals are included.

Some magazines have their own indexes, but you will save time by using the two above as they do index most of the important periodicals.

6. HOW LONG SHOULD AN ARTICLE BE?

The length of the article really depends upon the needs of the market, as well as on the subject matter itself. The market lists that you find in writers' magazines and yearbooks will give the number of words required. Usually they give a minimum and maximum number of words, such as "1,000 to 4,000 words."

This actually gives you plenty of workable space for your article. Knowing in advance what your length limit is will help to keep you "on target."

Often an editor, when buying from a query letter, will specify how many words he wants.

7. WHAT KIND OF VOCABULARY SHOULD I USE IN ARTICLES?

The vocabulary you use depends upon the type of article that you are writing and the kind of readership that the magazine for which you are preparing the article has.

A medical article for a medical or scientific journal will use a different vocabulary than a medical article written for a popular family magazine.

You should slant your vocabulary toward the type of market which you are aiming for. Research your market first.

8. WHY IS RESEARCH SO IMPORTANT IN ARTICLES?

Articles are "non-fiction," which means that they are not fantasy or imaginary but based on reality and fact. Your research is your foundation upon which you build your article.

Not all articles require extensive research. Some may require very little while others may mean months of work behind the scenes before you ever start writing.

An article based on your personal experiences will probably require less, if any, research, but an article based on what another perosn is doing or has done means digging into the subject matter in greater depth. An historical, medical, scientific or technical article usually requires more comprehensive research.

Before you write your article, you should have at least some idea of what facts you need and how much research is involved. You should actually know this before you send your query letter. It is embarrassing to have an article accepted and then discover that you can not finish the assignment because you can't complete your research!

9. WHAT ARE SOME OF THE REFERENCE BOOKS THAT I WILL NEED TO USE?

Your reference books will be directly tied to your choice of subject material. If you are a specialist in any subject, then you will be using books on that particular subject. However, there are certain basic books that can be used by an article writer no matter what his or her subject. Some of these books you will probably want to own (SEE Section 15), but for many of them you will depend upon your local library. The Reference Department of the public library and/or college library in your area is your most valuable source of information. A library card is as important a tool to you as your typewriter.

Get acquainted with these basic reference books: encyclopedias, dictionaries, atlases, and almanacs.

There are general encyclopedias and there are encyclopedias on almost any subject. Two of the best known encyclopedias are *The Encyclopedia Britannica* and *The Encyclopedia Americana*. There are many others and your library will probably have them in addition to the two I have listed. Each encyclopedia has an Index Volume which you can use to locate the information that you need.

Dictionaries are numerous in the reference field. There are dictionaries of language and there are dictionaries of subjects. We are all familiar with language dictionaries. The library will have several, including the large unabridged dictionaries. They will probably also have the famous *Oxford English Dictionary* which gives the complete history of our English language words. But there are also dictionaries of dates, artists, musicians, history, biography — just to mention a few. These are books on one subject, listed in an A to Z arrangement, usually with short entries, but in some cases they may contain as much information as an encyclopedia article.

Atlases also come in a variety of sizes and subjects. There are general atlases and atlases on special subjects, such as history, commerce and the military.

Almanacs are major sources of facts, chronologies of events and statistics. No matter what the subject, the almanacs will be able to provide you with needed facts and figures. One of the best known almanacs is *The World Almanac & Book of Facts*.

Every subject has its own special reference tools. You should become familiar with reference books in the fields in which you are writing.

Don't overlook the reference possibilities in newspapers and magazines. A paper like *The New York Times* is an invaluable reference source. Popular news magazines like *Time* and *Newsweek* will also have articles that can be used for reference.

There is one reference tool that you will always want to have access to — government publications. Your library may be a government depository for publications. If it is not, find out where your nearest government depository is and make use of it. Each week the government puts out pamphlets, leaflets and books on every conceivable subject. For instance, in a recent list of publications there was information on outdoor recreation, camping, the Shakers, the brown spider, alcoholism, consumer problems, energy conservation, various physical and mental health topics and many other subjects. To help you use this government material there are various indexes.

As an article writer, you will find many uses for quotations from famous people, both dead and contemporary. There are a number of good quotation books that you will find in the library. In addition you will find quotation books for some particular subjects, such as the *Bible* or Shakespeare.

Using your reference books wisely is like having a whole staff of research experts at your beck and call. Research can make the difference between a good article and one that just doesn't make it! The time you spend doing reference work is simply another way of increasing your article sales.

10. HOW DO I MAKE A REFERENCE SHEET?

A reference sheet is the best way to keep track of where you have looked for information and what you have found. This will keep you from repeating unnecessary steps and from forgetting what you may have found. It is also useful in rechecking facts and figures.

Take any sheet of paper or have a notebook and use it for a reference checklist sheet. For example, your sheet might look something like this:

                    Von Riventhro, Eric — Painter
x TIME Jan. 4, 1967 (Port + Life story + illus of work) p. 13-19
0 NEW YORKER
x NEWSWEEK Feb. 9, 1967 (Intv. + illus of work) p. 26-30
x NY TIMES INDEX (Sev. ref. 1949-69)
x ART IN AMERICA Jan. 1968 (Intv. + illus of work) p. 108
0 ART NEWS

If you think that you will need this information again, keep it in your reference file. Date it so that you will know at what period you did the original work. In any case, keep it until your article is published. It is very upsetting to get a call from an editor asking you about some fact in an article and not be able to recall where you found the information!

11. DO I HAVE TO BE ABLE TO PROVE THE FACT OR FIGURES THAT I USE?

Yes, and the burden of proof is on you! Editors expect you to be responsible about facts and figures. Sometimes they require proof either on a separate sheet or indicated in the article.

Keep your reference sheet (SEE Section 10) in the file with the completed article. You never know when you are going to be asked to substantiate some fact or figure. Even after the article is in print, there may be some questions raised about statistics or quotations.

Don't make up facts, statistics or other figures. There are plenty of sources for authentic facts and figures.

12. WHAT ABOUT THE DANGERS OF LIBEL, INVASION OF PRIVACY, ETC.?

As the writer, you are responsible for what you say in your articles. Although you have more freedom in writing about an individual who is a well-known public figure, your writing must not be libelous or you might become involved in a lawsuit. Whenever you write about a person, you must not only be accurate and sure of your facts, but you also have to be able to prove them if the matter is questioned.

The question of invasion of privacy is very much in the news these days. A tasteless article about an individual which is irrelevant to any current situation might well be considered an invasion of privacy and grounds for legal action.

The question of invasion of privacy is very much in the new these days. A tasteless article about an individual which is irrelevant to any current situation might well be considered an invasion of privacy and grounds for legal action.

Do get permission in writing before using photographs of people or quoting from letters, diaries or other privately-owned material.

By the way, you will also need permission to quote material of any length from a previously published work. Although there is no specific rule about how much may be quoted without permission, it is generally accepted that only small portions may be used without permission. Occasionally a book will stipulate what amounts may be used without getting written permission. If there are any doubts in your mind, it is best to write to the publisher and describe your project and indicate how much and what portions you wish to reprint. Most publishers are happy to give their permission provided that you give them credit in your article or book.

13. WHAT IS THE "MILLION DOLLAR FILE" AND HOW DO I MAKE ONE?

The "Million Dollar File" is one of your basic research tools. It is relatively inexpensive to make and keep up. You need the following: A file cabinet, file folders, scissors, marking pen, magazines and newspapers.

This file is your clipping file. As you read newspapers and magazines, you will come across articles, statistics, biographical sketches and other valuable information. If you do not want to keep the entire issue, simply cut out the section you want and file it.

File your clippings by subject. You will probably discover that your subjects will depend upon the kind of article that you write. For example, a travel writer will have a file which gives information about the life and customs in various countries. He will also probably have files on cities, modes of travel, restaurants, etc. A psychology-oriented writer's files will have headings like these: Depression, Family Life, Adolescence, and so on.

Mark the subject on your folders and file in alphabetical order. Mark the date of the paper or magazine on the clipping and the name of the periodical if it does not appear on the clipping itself. Small clippings can be pasted on a sheet of typing paper to keep them from getting lost.

Newspapers are an invaluable source of current statistics and other facts. In addition to your local paper or papers, you should subscribe to at least one city paper if you do not live in a large city. If you can not get daily papers, at least get the Sunday edition of some large metropolitan area newspaper.

These clippings are also useful for ideas. Very often you will be stimulated to think of an article by reading some statistics or some account of an event.

At least every five years you should go through your file and weed out material which is no longer relevant or accurate.

When you have a magazine that you could use in your research but don't want to cut it apart, you should index it. (SEE Section 14.)

14. HOW CAN I INDEX MAGAZINES THAT I DON'T WANT TO CUT UP?

You may subscribe to some magazines that you wish to keep in their entirety, yet they may contain valuable material that should be in your clipping file. You can, however, keep your magazines intact and still have your material readily accessible. All you have to do is to prepare your own index.

While it is true that some magazines have printed indexes and a great many are indexed in the large printed commercial indexes, that material is not available as soon as the magazine comes out. What you as an article writer need is a current, working reference tool.

It is easy to index your magazines. You will need some 3" × 5" file cards and a card holder. You can either type or write your cards. If you write them, be sure that they are easy to read so that when you go back in a few months you will know what you meant!

On the card you will need the following information:
        Subject
        Title of article
        Name of magazine
        Number of issue
        Page numbers

You may also want to add other pertinent information, such as: Has Bibliography, Includes Charts, or Genealogy. As a working writer, you know best what kinds of information you will be looking for.

Here is a sample card:
                      HEART
        "Closing In On The Causes Of Heart Trouble"
            FAMILY HEALTH, Jan. 1983, p. 15-17

Remember, you don't have to index everything in the issue — just those articles that you think you might want to refer to later.

Keep your cards in a file box and keep them up-to-date. It is very frustrating to have to look through a whole pack of cards when you need something in a hurry. File your cards alphabetically using guide cards to separate the different sections. In addition to the A — Z guide cards, you may want to use subject guide cards for subjects that you use most often. For example, your guide cards might look like this:

MEDICINE
MONEY
MYTHS

You can buy printed A — Z guide cards and use blank guide cards for the subject heading guides which are needed for your file.

15. WHAT BOOKS SHOULD I HAVE IN MY PERSONAL LIBRARY?

The number and kind of books that you have in your personal reference library will depend upon what kind of reference work you need to do and how extensive your research for articles has to be. It will also depend upon what access you have to other libraries in your area.

There are, however, some basic books which you will probably want to have in your personal library. Here are some titles that I recommend: *Writer's Market, The Writer's Handbook, The World Almanac & Book of Facts, Webster's Dictionary of Proper Names, Bartlett's Familiar Quotations.*

You will also want a good dictionary and a good atlas. Fortunately, many reference books today are also available in paperback editions so that your outlay of money will be considerably less than buying only clothbound books.

It is important that you keep your personal reference collection up to date by buying the latest issue of an almanac or yearbook.

16. CAN I REALLY SELL MY ARTICLES?

Yes — if you are willing to take the time to turn out a good piece of writing which is competently researched and well-presented both in style and in physical format.

Don't expect to sell articles which simply rehash old ideas or issues. Bait your hook with an angle that's different.

Send your queries to the right magazines. Don't waste your time trying to sell to the wrong markets. Read the editorial requirements and/or study the publication before submitting.

And don't overlook the trade journals, denominational magazines or the special interest magazines and papers. Writers do make a living selling to these smaller or special markets. Yes, it's wonderful to sell to *Playboy, The Atlantic,* or *The New Yorker,* but while waiting for that big sale, why not make a lot of small sales? They may even add up to more in the long run!

Regional publications as well as local papers and magazines are another source of article sales. Get acquainted with your local editors and publishers. When you are starting out, you may even be willing to do some articles for free or for a nominal fee. Each time that you are published adds to your experience. The time will come when you can move from the local paper or magazine to the regional and then to national publications. Remember that starting at the top is not the important thing, but it is the act of starting your professional career that counts! Remember also that there is a lot of satisfaction to be gained from being a local or regional writer. You may not get the highest rates of pay for your work, but you will have something more valuable — recognition and admiration from the people among whom you live. And who knows when a national syndicate is going to come around and pick up that weekly column or series for publication? Many famous writers started out in small ways!

17. SHOULD I WRITE THE ARTICLE FIRST OR TRY AND SELL THE IDEA FIRST

It is more practicle and sensible to try and sell your idea first by using the query letter. Why spend your time in writing and typing an article which may or may not sell when, with less time and effort and expense, you can prepare a query letter and outline?

Often, too, an editor will have specific requests or requirements which he wants to see brought out in the article. If you have already written the article, this means time-consuming revision and rewriting.

18. WHAT IS A QUERY LETTER, AND HOW DO I PREPARE ONE?

A query letter is your "bait." It should be prepared with the same care and thoroughness that you use on articles. In your query letter, give in brief form your idea for an article. Cover all the important points. Indicate whether or not illustrations will be available.

Give some of your writing credits and any information about your qualifications to write the particular article you are suggesting. This is particularly important if it is a technical or specialized subject.

You may, if you prefer, submit your query as an outline on a separate piece of paper and have a covering letter.

Always enclose a self-addressed stamped envelope.

Be sure that you have enough research material and information to write the article if the editor approves your idea.

Finally, send your letter addressed to an editor by name. You can find his or her name in your market lists or in a copy of the magazine or newspaper itself.

19. CAN I SEND A QUERY OR AN ARTICLE TO MORE THAN ONE PLACE AT THE SAME TIME?

Although multiple submissions are done by many writers, I always say "no" to this question. While it is true that multiple submissions save time, what happens when more than one editor likes your idea? It is embarrassing to have to write and say that the article has already been sold to another magazine. The next time you want to send a query to that editor, he will probably remember his past experience with you and you may not get the kind of consideration and interest from him that you want.

The best way is to have several ideas, make up queries and send them out, each one to a different editor.

The only exception to this general rule of individual one-at-a-time submissions is when you send to a highly specialized periodical that has a limited and self-contained circulation. For example, you might sell an article on Easter customs to two different religious denominational magazines since it is obvious that their readership is widely separated. However, you would have to be sure that each editor understood that you were doing this.

20. WHERE CAN I FIND MARKET INFORMATION?

Special publications issued for writers are major sources of market information. These publications include monthly magazines as well as annual volumes.

The magazines are: *The Writer, Writer's Digest.*

Both of these magazines have news each month about markets for articles, latest news about magazines and features that will help you in your writing. In addition, once a year *The Writer* publishes a special listing of markets for specialized articles and a list of markets for general articles. During the year they also publish lists on trade journals, recreational magazines and other possible article markets.

Also invaluable as sources for market news are: *Writer's Market, Writer's Yearbook,* and *The Writer's Handbook.*

You will want to have the latest editions of these books. You should have them in your personal library, but if you can not get them, most libraries have copies in their reference departments.

Another source of market information comes from your own reading of newspapers and magazines. By studying what they are publishing, you know whether or not you have something which might interest them.

21. DO I HAVE TO READ ALL THE MAGAZINES TO WHICH I SUBMIT ARTICLES?

No, but you will certainly want to be familiar with them. You will want to keep up on the magazines which are in your special field if you have one subject that you devote much of your time to.

Regular visits to your public library's periodical collection will help you keep abreast of what is being published in current issues. Another good source is the *Reader's Digest* since it publishes articles from many magazines in each issue.

When you go to a newsstand, scan the covers of the magazines which most interest you. Usually, the lead articles are featured on the cover. You can decide then if you want to purchase an issue for your files.

In No. 13 we discussed how to make the best use of the magazines and papers that you buy.

Remember that one of the reasons you keep up with what is being published is so that you don't waste time trying to sell a similar article to the same market.

22. DO I NEED AN AGENT?

Yes and no! Yes, an agent would probably be of assistance in placing articles and in getting you higher prices for them. No, because you can sell your articles yourself.

Remember that agents are interested in writers who sell and who have made a name and reputation for themselves. The beginner has to prove to an agent that he can do it.

An agent collects a 10% or 15% commission. When you start out, most of your sales will probably be to the smaller markets where the pay may be only in the under $100 range. You can be very happy selling to a dozen such markets, but the agent would feel that it was hardly worth his while.

When you become more successful, then you can decide whether or not you want to have an agent. And the more successful you are, the more willing an agent is to handle you!

23. SHOULD I USE MY REAL NAME OR A PSEUDONYM?

A lot depends on what kind of articles you are writing. If you are, for example, writing medically-oriented articles and you are a doctor, nurse or psychologist, you will want to use your own name because you are known in that field. The same applies to any other type of professional writing, whether you are an architect, engineer or teacher.

If you are a professional writer writing on a variety of subjects, then you may want to use your own name for certain articles and other names for other articles. One writer I know writes historical material under his own name, travel articles under one pseudonym, and articles on food and gourmet cooking under still another name. There have been times when all three of his names were on articles in a single issue of a magazine!

Whatever names you use in addition to your own or instead of your own, stick with them. You want editors to get familiar with the name or names you are using.

24. HOW MUCH REWRITING DO I NEED TO DO?

Since you will probably write most of your articles either as direct assignments or speculation pieces, most of the rewriting that you do will probably be at the request of an editor.

It is always best to be cooperative with editors for you will find that they usually know what their readers want.

25. WHY ARE TITLES SO IMPORTANT?

When you send in your query letter and outline, you will also send along a title for your article. Now, the editor may later change that title, but initially it is part of your "bait" to get the editor interested in the article.

You want to use titles that are descriptive, catchy, easy to understand and provocative. A title, when it appears in a table of contents, has to catch the reader's eye. It has to make him want to turn to that page and read the article. Contrast these three titles:

>"*Automobile Statistics*"
>"*Automobile Statistics Reveal Startling Facts*"
>"*Death Rides with You*"

The first title is not very good; in fact, it is dull. The second title is better but the third is the best of the three. It is an attention getter!

Be sure that your title fits your article. Readers resent it when they have been promised something in a title which is not delivered in the article itself.

26. HOW CAN I FIND OUT THE PUBLICATION SCHEDULE OF A MAGAZINE?

Most magazines work on schedules which are far in advance of actual publication dates. Their May issue may be on the newsstands, but in the editorial offices they are working on the December issue.

Knowing the publication schedules and editorial deadlines is particularly important if you are submitting seasonal material.

Write to the magazine and ask for the times in which they are working on the various issues. Keep this information in your files so that you know when to submit seasonal material. You may get inspired to write an article on winter sports in December, but most periodicals are already past that period editorially speaking. So you will have to wait for the right time to submit it or send it to a magazine or newspaper which has a much shorter time span between editorial work and actual publication.

27. WHAT ABOUT ARTICLES WRITTEN IN COLLABORATION WITH OTHER PEOPLE?

There are times when you may find it best to have a joint author. An article written in collaboration may sell better if your collaborator is an expert in the field. If, for instance, you have an idea for an article for an architectural magazine, you might want to get a well-known architect to be your collaborator. Or, if you have an idea for a medical article for the popular market, a doctor-collaborator would be helpful.

In the case of collaboration, both names should appear on the article and the money received for the article should be divided 50-50 unless you have made other arrangements.

Some professional people are happy to help you out with technical facts and information without authorship credit or payment. There are times, however, when a collaborator's name, profession or reputation may help to sell your article.

28. WHAT ABOUT THE "AS TOLD TO" ARTICLES?

"As told To" articles are somewhat similar to collaborative articles. However, these articles are clearly the authorship of the writer with the facts and background being supplied by the other person. Usually the other person is someone who has had a dramatic or unusual experience but is unable to write about that experience.

A typical title would be "Lost In The Mountains For Thirty-One Days" by James Foote As Told By Alice Smith.

Usually the narrator is paid part of the money received for the article. You should make all financial arrangements before writing and submitting the article. Have your arrangements written on paper and signed by both yourself and the other party to the agreement. A verbal agreement can be strained to the breaking point during the writing period or after publication.

29. DO I NEED ILLUSTRATIONS FOR MY ARTICLES?

Whether or not you should have illustrations depends largely upon two factors: one, the kind of article and two, the kind of market to which you are selling.

Many articles are enhanced by photographs or drawings. for instance, a travel article or an article on home decoration depends a great deal on its illustrations for its reader interest and therefore its salability in the first place.

If you aren't interested in taking your own photographs or just happen to be "all thumbs" with even the simplest camera, try forming a professional relationship with a free-lance photographer. Together, you and your photographer may be able to have a winning combination.

But, if you are going to be your own photographer, be sure that the photographs you send with your articles are truly professional ones. Be sure that your photographs are properly identified and include captions with them. The captions can be typed and fasted to the bottom of the photographs, be careful not to cover up any of the photograph or damage it in any way. *Writer's Market* has a sample photographic model release form to follow. You may also need permission if you want to use a photograph of a private residence or a building. Usually people are glad to be cooperative and thrilled to be in an article. It is best to be sure in advance however. It is always a good policy to give people a copy of the article in which a photograph for which they have given permission appears.

30. HOW SHOULD MY ARTICLE MANUSCRIPT BE TYPED?

Type on standard white 8½" × 11" typing paper. Always double-space and stay away from script type. Be sure that your ribbon is good and your type clean. A faintly typed manuscript or one with the letters filled in has little chance of being read. All corrections should be neatly made and if a sheet has too many, type it over!

On the first page, type your name and address in the upper left corner and type the title about one-third of the way down the page.

William Goteez
219 W. 4th St.
Santa Fe, New Mexico 87501
Tel. (505) 473-2688

HAPPINESS IS YOUR RIGHT

Happiness is just as much a right as is any other hard-won political or social right. We have let ourselves down by accept-

On the succeeding pages, type your last name and a key phrase from the title and put this in the upper left corner.

Be sure that you have numbered each page. You may number in the upper right or bottom center.

A word count should be put in the upper right corner on the first page. It can be an approximate count ("About 3,000 words").

Always be sure that you have a carbon copy of your article.

31. HOW SHOULD I MAIL MY MANUSCRIPT AND WHAT SHOULD I INCLUDE?

Mail your manuscript first class. It is worth the extra money be sure that it gets there promptly. If you have to meet a deadline and the time is short, send your manuscript express mail or by one of the overnight private couriers such as Purolator.

You should keep your pages together with a paper clip. If you fasten the clip over a small piece of paper, you will avoid marking your copy.

Mail in a manila envelope. If you are enclosing photographs, add cardboard to help protect them and mark your envelope DO NOT BEND.

If this is an article which has been ordered, you do not have to include any return envelope or return postage. However, be sure to include a letter to the editor stating that in response to his request you are sending the article on___. This is particulary helpful if some time has elapsed since the initial correspondence with the editor. It will refresh his memory. Also, if there has been a change at the magazine, the editor receiving it will know its history.

If you are sending out an article instead of the usual query letter, include a letter which tells your qualifications to write this article and gives some of your writing background, other publications, etc.

Always address your manuscript to the editor with whom you have corresponded. If this is being sent in "cold," address it to one of the editors. You can get a name from either your market list or from the publication itself. Always include a self-addressed, stamped return envelope. Your envelope should be the right size for your manuscript.

32. HOW LONG SHOULD I WAIT FOR A REPLY FROM AN EDITOR?

The length of time that you have to wait usually depends upon whether or not the magazine to which you submit work has a large enough staff to handle all submissions promptly. Also, in some of the magazines, a decision on acceptance of an article or query must come from more than one person.

However, I'd say a reasonable time would be 6 to 8 weeks. If you have not heard by then, I would send a brief, polite letter of inquiry to the editor.

If you get no answer to your inquiry, send a registered letter and, at that time if you so desire, indicate that you are withdrawing your manuscript or query.

When waiting for a manuscript, be sure to take into account the fact that it takes the manuscript several days from the time it leaves your hands until it reaches its destination, particularly if you are sending from one coast to the other.

33. WHAT DOES "ON SPECULATION" MEAN?

An editor may reply to a query letter by asking you if you are willing to write an article on speculation. This means that he is not saying yes nor is he saying no. For one reason or another, he wants to see the finished article before making a final editorial decision.

It's up to you to decide whether or not you want to invest the time and trouble in an unsure thing. Unless you are terribly busy, it is probably wise to go ahead and do it. If he does reject it, you can always try somewhere else.

34. WHAT ABOUT RIGHTS?

When you sell an article, you sell the "rights" to it. However, there are various rights that can be bought.

"All Rights" means just that — the magazine owns all the rights. The writer can not use that material elsewhere, although sometimes he can get remaining rights back or permission to use the article in a book.

"First Serial Rights" means that the periodical has the right to be the first to publish the article. Other rights belong to the author but must be assigned in writing to him.

There are also "Second Serial Rights," "Reprint Rights" and "Simultaneous Rights." Second Serial Rights can mean either the second publication of an article in a periodical after it has already appeared in another magazine, or it can mean the serial publication of parts of a book in a magazine or newspaper.

Some magazines will buy material which has appeared in other publications (Reprint Rights), but be sure that you have the right to sell your article twice.

Occasionally, magazines which have specialized circulations will buy articles which are going to appear in another magazine at the same time. Technical, denominational and some fraternal magazines do this.

When you sell an article, be sure that you are aware of what rights you are selling and which ones, if any, you are keeping.

35. WHAT KIND OF RECORDS SHOULD I KEEP?

Once you get started on your professional writing career there should be a constant flow of articles in and out of your "office" and you will need to keep accurate records on what you are doing.

Actually, you will need two files, one an "Outlines" file and one for recording the in and out movement of your articles.

Your file of outlines should be on 5" x 8" cards. The card should contain the complete query outline (use two cards if necessary). The title of the article and the date the outline was first written should be on the top line. Above your title should be the subject. All cards are to be filed by this subject heading. On the back of your card write the headings OUTLINES and ARTICLES. Under OUTLINES list the date when and name of the magazine to which you have sent the outline. If it accepts your outline, list the name of the magazine and date of acceptance under the other column. When you have sold a query, put a mark of some kind or a colored self-stick dot on the face of your card. When looking through your file, you will know at a quick glance which outlines have been sold. If you revise an outline, type a new card and clip it in front of the old card.

A typical card might look like this:

(front)

JUVENILE DELINQUENCY   1/5/84

How One Neighborhood Has Successfully Handled Juvenile Crime

The suburb of Ritchie, N.C. has long been harrased by a juvenile crime problem. Two years ago in the wake of a teen-age

(back)

OUTLINES	*ARTICLES*
1/5/84 Nat. Monthly	*2/25/84 Nat. Monthly*

Another file of 5" × 8" cards should be used to keep track of submissions, sales, etc. This can be arranged by the title of your article. On this card should be listed the following information: name of magazine or other buyer, number of words in article, date sent in, date payment received and amount of any expenses incurred in writing the article, postage expenses, rights purchased and date of issue in which article is published. This information card can give you all the facts you need about the business end of your article writing career.

If you write an article on speculation and it is not accepted, that fact should be entered on the card and the name of the second place to which you sent it, etc.

These cards are the "life histories" or your articles. They are helpful to you in preparing income tax statements, in assessing the success of your own career and in keeping tabs on the payment of monies and the publication of your articles.

36.   HOW CAN I USE A TAPE RECORDER?

A tape recorder is invaluable in helping you with your interviews. It frees you to concentrate on talking and listening to your subject. Many people "freeze up" when they see their words written down. With a tape recorder in use, you need to make only a few notes as reminders. There is another advantage to using a tape recorder — it enables you to have accurate quotations. You don't have to guess what the individual said; you can check back on your tape and quote exactly what was said.

If you do research in a library carrell or other private place, you may want to record your findings on your tape recorder rather than write them down.

37.   HOW SHOULD I PREPARE FOR THE PERSONAL INTERVIEW?

Very often you will find that you will want to have personal interviews in order to get facts or background for an article. In some cases, your entire article is being based on the life, profession or view of the person being interviewed.

Here is a check list of pre-interview duties:
1. Call the individual and set up a time and place.
2. Be sure that he or she understands what you want and what you are going to do with your information.
3. If pictures are needed, either ask the interviewee to provide some and have them ready or ask permission to take pictures.
4. Tell the person in advance if you are going to tape the interview.
5. Before going, try to find out as much information as you can about the interviewee. If he or she is a public or quasi-public figure, visit the public library and look though issues of the local paper. Most libraries keep up an index on local notables. If he is an artist and shows in a gallery, visit the gallery and become familiar with his work. If he has written anything, read it before the interview.
6. Prepare an outline of the questions you want to ask.
7. Be sure all of your equipment (recorder, camera, etc.) is in working order before you go.
8. Have enough pens or pencils and paper.
9. Be on time for your appointment!

38. HOW SHOULD I CONDUCT A PERSONAL INTERVIEW?

Put the interviewee at ease by talking about generalities while you set up your recorder, get out your pencils, etc. You may wonder why you need to take notes when you are also recording. I have found that most people feel reassured if they see you taking notes. You do not have to take complete notes when you also have a recorder. The tape recorder also prevents any error in using quotations.

Remind the interviewee of the purpose of the interview and how it is going to be used.

Put the interviewee further at ease by commenting on his work, his philosophy or some other personal matter. Do not start the actual interview abruptly. Never lose your patience with an interviewee even if he tends to wander from the subject of the interview.

Using your questions that have been previously prepared, start the interview. Listen closely to the replies. They may give you clues to other questions you should ask or leads you should follow up.

If the interviewee is elderly or in poor health, watch for any sign of fatigue and terminate the interview. In any case, do not make any interview too long. If you have many things to cover, it might be better to have two interviews with the person. This has to be left to your judgement.

If your interviewee supplies you with pictures, find out if they need to be returned. Be sure you understand what the pictures are and write down that information at the time of the interview. If you are having pictures taken, you may want to have the interviewee sign a model's release.

You have to use a lot of your intuitive thinking when on an interview. Each person is different and only you can determine how that individual should be treated.

Some people want to see your written copy before it is submitted for publication. If the interviewee does request this, comply and discuss amicably any changes he would like made.

When the material is printed, you should return any borrowed pictures. It is always a good idea to give copies of any pictures that you have taken. This is just a good will gesture. See that the interviewee gets either a copy of the printed article or, if that is not possible, at least knows when and where it was published.

39. CAN I EVER PUBLISH MY ARTICLES IN BOOK FORM?

You can if: 1. There is a demand for them and 2. You get permission from the periodicals in which they first appeared.

A book should have a unifying theme and not be just a hodgepodge of reprints. For example, if you have written and had published a series of articles on the effects of the energy crisis on the environment, a publisher might be interested in bringing them out in book form. It is sometimes best to have some additional unpublished material to add to the book.

If you have a series of articles that you think might be good for a book, write a publisher a query. List the articles and where they were published, indicate any new material that could be added and send at least two reprints or copies of published articles with your letter. You can find names and addresses of publishers in your market lists.

If the publisher says "yes" and sends a contract, find out if he or you are responsible for writing to the various periodicals for permission to reprint.

40. WHY WOULD HAVING PRINTED STATIONERY OR BUSINESS CARDS HELP MY IMAGE?

If you are trying to make this a serious business or full-time career, you will find it useful to have business stationery and business cards.

Printed stationery does make a good impression on an editor. It is also an ego builder for you. Business cards are useful when you are looking for information, asking for an interview or trying to meet an editor.

All of these help to reinforce your own self-image as a professional writer.

41. WHAT ARE THE SECRETS BEHIND A SUCCESSFUL ARTICLE?

There is no magic formula for articles but there are some practical rules that you can follow that will help you achieve successful publication.

Keep your audience in mind. Don't talk down and don't sermonize. I always suggest that you write as if you were talking to one particular person. Visualize that person seated across the desk from you or sitting in a chair by your side. This will personalize your article. You want each reader to feel that you are talking to him or to her.

Start out with a blockbuster sentence! You have to get your reader's attention immdediately. He has to read that first sentence and then be led into the rest of the article. Don't start out with a low-keyed or dull tone. You want to reach out and grab the reader!

Contrast these two versions of an opening sentence:

"*Statisticians say that over 50,000 persons die each year in automobile accidents.*"

"*Will you be one of the 50,000 Americans to die this year because of your automobile?*"

As you can see, the second sentence has more personal impact.

Your whole article has to be so constructed that one sentence leads to another. You can't afford to lose a reader at any point in your article. You want to keep him interested until the very end. Your final paragraph should be a conclusion that leaves your reader completely satisfied with what he has read. Hopefully, it will also make him want to see articles written by you!

PLAYS

Playwriting is one of the fundamental ways in which man expresses his ideas and feelings. Plays, not perhaps as we know them today, but ideas in dramatic form were acted out long before anyone ever thought of writing them down.

It is natural to act. Watch children and see how they enjoy acting out situations. When they are playing make-believe, they are, unconsciously, acting. As children grow older, they usually go through a period in which they consciously act out little plays for their own amusement, for their peers, or for their parents and other adults.

Most adults become too self-conscious to continue to enjoy playing at acting, except perhaps at parties when they play charades. But the enjoyment and appreciation of the dramatic remains, and so we have audiences for our plays, movies and television.

In this chapter I will try to answer some of the questions that beginning playwrights have asked me. I hope that it will be a helpful and useful book as well as an inspiring one for you.

The playwright has a long tradition — he has always been a part of the human scene — needed to record in dramatic form the history, the feelings and the aspirations of the human race.

1. WHAT QUALITIES DO I NEED AS A PLAYWRIGHT?

You will need to be aware of other people, their attitudes and responses to events and their relationships with others. You will need to have an acute awareness of situations.

You will want to study people (without being too obvious, of course) to try and discover what makes them the way they are and, in particular, what makes them respond the way they do.

You will need patience and dedication. Writing plays is not easy work. It may be fun (and should be) in many ways, but it still means hours of hard work. Your rewards may be on the slim side and it may take you a long time to get established.

As a playwright you will want to develop the habit of regarding your experiences as a series of scenes. You will always be on the lookout for dramatic conflict and resolution, for good characters and for dramatic ideas.

2.   WHAT KIND OF PLAYS SHOULD I WRITE?

If by what kind of plays you mean whether or not you should write comedies or tragedies, the answer lies within yourself. How do you look at life? Are you inclined to be very serious? Or do you see the humorous side of life?

How do you regard people? Do you see them as acting out some awesome drama that we call life, or do you perceive the lighter side, or the irony of people's relationships to life and to each other?

The way in which you see and relate to life and to other people is probably going to determine the first play that you write. But, as you go on and get more experience, you may very well change from comedies to tragedies or vice versa. In the long run you will make a choice because you are most comfortable with a certain form and because you will recognize what is appropriate for the play idea itself. Some ideas and some situations demand serious treatment while others would be ruined by being presented seriously.

Making people laugh is a great challenge. and don't overlook the fact that serious ideas can be treated in comedies.

You may also wonder whether you should write one-act, two-act or three-act plays. Again, the more experienced you are, the more you will be able to realize just what a play calls for. You may be able to say all you should in one act. On the other hand, some ideas requre a longer time to properly develop characters and work out solutions to conflicts.

If you are a beginner, I'd suggest starting with the one-act play. It is a little easier to handle. You will be less likely to put in too much extraneous material, and the discipline of the one act will force you to concentrate on your dramatic idea.

3. WHERE DO I GET IDEAS FOR PLAYS?

Ideas are everywhere. If they were visible objects, you'd be falling over them!

As a playwright you have many sources on which to draw for dramatic ideas. For example, there's your own life and your family. Many famous and well-known playwrights use their own experiences as a springboard for plays. Eugene O'Neill is one who comes readily to mind.

You are always surrounded by dramatic situations. You only have to learn to recognize them as containing the seeds for a play. Remember that you are not necessarily going to visualize the entire play. What you will look for is the germ, the beginning, and from that you will create your play.

History is another rich source of ideas for plays, but you will have to do research. Your historical play can be built around a single historical episode or be based on the impact of an idea or belief on history. You may want to write a play that centers around an historical figure. There have been hundreds of plays written about Lincoln, for example. If you do write a play about a popular historical person, you will want to be sure that your play has something different to say. If not, you won't be able to hold the attention of your audience. People don't want to hear and see the same old story over and over.

Novels and stories are other sources for play ideas. It is a real art to take a novel or story and transfer it to the stage. You have to be sure that there are dramatic possibilities inherent in the original book or story. From a practical point of view, you also have to get permission to do this unless, of course, you are simply doing it as an exercise in developing your skill, or as an aid to break a mental block.

4. ARE THERE SOME SUBJECTS THAT SHOULDN'T BE HANDLED IN DRAMA?

In theory, almost any subject can be put into some kind of dramatic form, but not every subject is going to be successful as drama. Because of the physical dimensions of the stage itself, a battle scene is less effective than a conversation between a few characters.

There are also some subjects that might be considered to be in bad taste. It is true that on today's stage almost "anything goes"; however, a great deal will depend upon where you expect your play to be performed. By keeping your possible audience in mind, you will be influenced to some extent in your choice of subject material.

5. HOW DO I START TO WRITE MY PLAY?

You start with your idea and then write a series of progressively more detailed synopses. At the same time, make a list of characters and their physical, mental and emotional characteristics, as well as their relationships to each other.

Your first synopsis will be very sketchy. For instance, it may read like this:

The Glass Beehive

A factory owner is accused of blighting the area ecologically. At the same time, the factory workers are demanding more pay and threaten to strike. He is pressured on the one hand by the environmentalists and on the other hand by the workers. An inventor comes up with an anti-pollution device, but its installation would change manufacturing methods and result in the need for fewer workers. No one wants to listen to the problems of the factory owner or help him find the right solution. To complicate matters, his personal life is affected by the fact that his wife sides with the environmentalists and has fallen in love with the inventor. Both the head of the environmentalist group and the head of the union are also in love, to some extent, with factory owner's wife. A possible ending would be that the factory owner turns the factory over to the union members and lets them fight it out with the environmentalists. He gives his wife an ultimatum and she has to make a choice between the inventor and himself. To everyone's surprise, she announces that she is going to stay with the union head. At the same time the workers announce that they will fight the environmentalists and throw the inventor out of town in order to save their jobs.

Subsequent synopses will go into more detail and finally you will have a synopsis which lists the action that occurs in each scene. This will be your working blueprint as you write the play. Now this doesn't mean that you can not make changes. Your play is organic and should grow naturally as you create it. Very often you will find that an action, a scene or a characterization that you have worked out in the preliminary synopsis does not work in the actual writing. Change whatever seems necessary.

Your character list will start out in the same way — very sketchy and broad. You will gradually narrow it down to finer details and specific characteristics. For example, you first list of characters may look like this:

The Glass Beehive

Factory Owner — Middle-aged, wealthy, conservative but anxious to do right.
Factory Owner's Wife — Middle-aged, still attractive, interested in "causes," restless and dissatisfied with her life — she thinks. Falls in love with inventor.
Inventor — Attractive, brilliant, not always practical.

Environmentalist Head — An idealist, perhaps in love to some extent with factory owner's wife.

Union Head — Torn between his duty to workers and his natural inclination toward making a better world. A bit in love with factory owner's wife.

The next character list that you make will go into more details as to physical characteristics and you will start to give your characters their names. They will then become not symbols, but "true-dimensional" flesh and blood people to you.

In this first synopsis and character list, what you have done is to delineate in broad strokes your characters and the basic action and areas of conflict in the play. You have also worked out the possible solution and resolution of those conflicts. This, of course, may change as you work on the play. Characters have a way of taking over and finding their own solutions. What you, the playwright, have to be sure of is that it is good logic and good theater.

You will also want to set your model stage (SEE No. 16) and probably also make a diagram of your setting on paper.

6. WHERE DO I GET MY CHARACTERS?

Characters, like ideas, are all around you. You only have to be alert and very observant of other people. Make it a practice to study people when you are in a group, waiting for an appointment, riding in a bus, train or airplane, or when you are part of an audience. Become a student of human nature!

Observe physical characteristics, facial expressions, gestures and posture. Look for the identifying physical characteristics that would best describe an individual. Ask yourself how you would relate these characteristics to the individual's personality. What do they reveal to you as a playwright and what can they reveal to an audience?

Observe actions. When you write a play, your characters are going to be moving about the stage. People move in different ways, ways that are influenced by situations, emotional reactions and physical limitations.

The characters that you create in your play must have the same attributes as any flesh and blood people have or you will fail to make them seem real to your audience. And you can not conceive of fully-rounded characters until you become adept at observing other people.

Naturally, the characters you create are not going to be carbon copies of all the people you meet or see. You will probably "assemble" your characters from bits and pieces of various people. You may "borrow" one individual's facial expression, another's gestures, and body characteristics from a third person. There is no limit upon your imagination and no limit to your source of raw material.

When you are particulary impressed by someone you meet or see and want to remember a gesture or an expression, make a note in your idea notebook (SEE No. 14). Your note might read like this: "X, when questioned, rubs his hand across the back of his neck." Or: "A. always bows slightly forward when shaking hands, almost a suggestion of curtsy. Gesture in keeping with her old-fashioned ideas."

All of the personal idiosyncrasies which you make notes of can be very useful in developing characterization. You may not use the information for a long time but, when you want it, it will be available.

There are times when your ideas for a particular character may be nebulous; however, reading through the ideas you have collected on people may help you to "see" what you need for that character.

For playwrights, "people-watching" can be very profitable!

7. HOW MUCH DO I NEED TO KNOW ABOUT MY CHARACTERS?

You need to know a great deal about the characters in your play. You need to know far more than your audience knows or wants to know. In the play, the characters appear for a set time. This time may be for a short period — an afternoon, a day or a weekend — or your play may encompass the passage of several years. It is rare that you are able to cover the entire span of a character's life and, in any case, you are limited to only certain specific scenes and actions.

Your characters, if they are to be believable, must behave during their times on stage as they would in real life. Therefore, their actions have to be consistent with those parts which are shown on the stage, but you, the playwright, must also have knowledge of that unseen portion of your character's lives. What you show in your play are the things that have been selected because they best portray the story. In other words, you know all about your characters, but you have to be selective in what you use dramatically.

The best and easiest way to become familiar with your characters is to write a brief biographical statement about each one. This will help you think of them as real people and keep them from becoming two-dimensional cardboard figures.

You should also have a clear picture in your mind of their physical characteristics. Write these down as well. You should make them more detailed than you will need for your final play script. I know one playwright who cuts pictures from newspapers and magazines of people whose features match up with the characters he is using. He says that these help him visualize his characters more easily.

Identify with your characters. Your task is very similar to that of the actor except that you must identify with all the characters rather than just one.

8. WHY IS DIALOGUE SO IMPORTANT AND HOW CAN I IMPROVE MY DIALOGUE?

Dialogue is the flesh of the play. It is through dialogue that you communicate with the audience. It is through dialogue that you present and resolve conflicts, show emotions and reactions and interpret human relationships.

You can improve your dialogue by listening to the way people talk. To make your characters realistic and believable, they must talk the way people in their circumstances would talk.

Listen with a playwright's ear to what you hear!

9. WHAT ARE SOME OF THE THINGS THAT I SHOULD KEEP IN MIND WHEN WRITING MY PLAYS?

It is well to keep in mind the physical limitations of the stage. You can, it is true, do a great deal with the aid of such devices as the revolving stage, split-staging and the clever use of physical space. New playwrights are sometimes influenced by motion pictures and try to do the impossible on the stage. The camera offers the dramatist unlimited scope but, on the other hand, the stage presents a real challenge. You have to work your material into the space you have. You have to make your audience so believe in what you are presenting to them that they forget the physical limitations of the stage.

When you are planning your set and the properties needed to successfully put on your play, be realistic about what is available to stage companies. A set calling for elaborate properties may present problems.

As budgetary costs rise, the one-set play is becoming more and more popular. And, if your play will stand it, you might suggest playing it with a minimum of scenery or with a rather stylized set. In any case, if your play is produced, the director and stage designer will decide just how your play is to be presented. If you see your play in terms of rather grandiose settings, just remind yourself occasionally that in Shakespeare's time, scenery and props were often minimal. One tree, for example, was used to represent an entire forest!

Also for budgetary costs, you will find that the play that calls for a small cast is usually preferred by many groups to the plays that have large casts. Leave the crowd scenes to the movies! When a play is to be presented by the local amateur theater, small casts are often preferred. For one thing, it is sometimes difficult to get enough people willing to give up time for rehearsals and performances. In addition, a play with fewer parts usually has parts of fairly equal value. In casting a local production it is important that each person feels that his part is vital to the success of the play.

It is a rare play that can succeed with a cast of all men or all women. Not only are there difficulties in casting such a play, especially in the amateur theater, but also the special themes that such plays present are difficult to handle. Most of them have already been done so ably that it would be difficult to outshine them. For instance *The Women* by Clare Boothe has become a classic example.

Animals on stage are always risky. You can not predict just how they will respond to an audience or what they will do. If you must have an animal on stage, make its appearance brief and in a situation where it can be controlled as part of the action. I have seen some good scenes ruined for the actors by the antics of stage animals.

Small children are also unpredictable. In writing a part for a child, keep in mind this unreliability. On the professional stage children's parts present no problem. But when you are writing for amateur or semi-professional companies, you will be very fortunate if they are able to get child actors who can give a good performance.

Although you as the playwright are mainly concerned with writing your play and putting your ideas into dramatic form, you have to look beyond the script to the demanding technical problems of production. If you are completely unrealistic about these problems, you will considerably lessen your chances of getting your plays produced.

10. HOW LONG SHOULD A PLAY BE?

A play should be as long as is needed to cover the action. However, you as the playwright, have to determine what is the best length for your play. A play can be too long to hold its audience. You can tell if your play is too long if you have to pad it out to get what you think is the required time.

A one-act play may be as short as 15 minutes or as long as an hour. Many one-act plays fall into the 25 to 35 minute range. But again, time really depends upon the subject to be covered and the amount of action in the play.

A three-act play usually lasts from two to three hours. This includes intermissions.

To begin with, don't worry about the length of your play. Just write what you feel is right for the play. When you have finished, you can check the time. Keep in mind that your reading time will be shorter and that, in actual production, time will be taken up with various bits of stage business.

11. SHOULD I READ THE WORKS OF OTHER DRAMATISTS?

Yes. After all, your interest in theater is not confined to just your own plays. For the same reason you should make it a habit to attend dramatic performances whenever you can. And today, even if you live in a town where there is little live theater, you can see some excellent professional theater on television, especially on the Public Broadcasting System channel.

In your reading, you should read the works of both past and contemporary dramatists. Read a play at least twice, once for the play itself and then again and perhaps several times for the dramatic techniques and the characterizations. Study the stage directions, the settings, the actions and how conflicts are introduced and resolved.

12. WHAT DRAMATISTS SHOULD I READ AND STUDY?

The greatest playwright, I think, is Shakespeare. You should be familiar with all of his plays. Don't be put off by what you may have read or studied in school. Read Shakespeare now as a fellow dramatist and a great mentor. See how he handled basic human conflicts and characterizations.

Here is a list of other playwrights with whose work you should become familiar. This list includes not only English and American playwrights but also foreign playwrights whose works have become part of our dramatic history. This list also includes some of the very first playwrights of importance.

Aristophanes	Euripides	Christopher Marlowe
Richard Sheridan	Anton Chekov	Henrik Ibsen
Maxwell Anderson	Bertolt Brecht	T.S. Eliot
Eugene O'Neill	Luigi Pirandello	George Bernard Shaw
Edward Albee	Samuel Beckett	Noel Coward
Christopher Fry	Lillian Hellman	Arthur Miller

Remember, these are only suggestions. You will discover, through reading and attending plays, certain dramatists that become your own favorites either because of their style or themes.

In addition to reading the works of dramatists, you will want to start your own play library with copies of the plays of your favorite authors. You can also augment your reading by studying other books about the theater and about the times of some of the famous earlier dramatists.

Biographies of playwrights and of actors and actresses will increase your knowledge of the theater and help you in your own writing.

13. WHAT BOOKS SHOULD I HAVE IN MY PERSONAL LIBRARY?

You will find it helpful to have at least some of the books and magazines for writers which are listed in No. 29 and in the Bibliography.

A good dictionary is invaluable. If you can get an unabridged one, fine. If not, get the next size that you can, such as *The American Heritage Dictionary of the English Language.*

Get a complete set of Shakespeare's plays, either in one volume or in several small volumes. Most of the plays are available in paperback editions.

As mentioned, you will probably want a collection of plays and biographies of your favorite dramatists.

A good history of the theater will not only give you background information, but will also serve as an inspiration to you. One title is *Plays, Players, & Playwrights* by Marion Geisinger (Hart Publishing Co., Inc.). An older one which you might be able to pick up secondhand is *The Theatre: Three Thousand Years of Drama, Acting and Stagecraft* by Sheldon Cheney. (Longmans, Green & Co.)

To help you with the technical side of your plays, you should have some books on stage designing, stage lighting, costuming, directing, etc.

To properly understand theater terms, you need some books that give clear and concise definitions and explanations. Two useful books are *Theatre Backstage From A to Z* by Warren C. Lounsbury (University of Washington Press) and *The Penguin Dictionary of the Theatre* by James Russel Taylor (Penguin Books).

Since books appear and then go out of print, the titles I have given here are offered only as examples and suggestions. There are new books on theater appearing every day. Go to your public or college library and to your book store and see what is available before making your final selection.

14. HOW CAN I USE AN IDEA NOTEBOOK?

You will get more ideas than you can use at any one time, but you will want to preserve the extra ones for future use. This is where your idea notebook comes in handy. Write your ideas down. Don't worry about whether or not they are complete or even seem to be useful at the time. The idea that appears useless now may be the very one you need sometime when you are stuck in a play.

I suggest getting a large size notebook, one that uses $8\frac{1}{2}$" 4 11" paper, and some notebook dividers. Keep your notes in sections. For instance, you will probably have a section on characters, one on plots, one on dialogue and one on settings. Add as many sections as you want.

You will use your idea notebook when working on a play, when you are temporarily bogged down or when you have run out of ideas.

And, as you read newspapers and magazines, cut out articles, news stories or fillers that have a place in your idea book. In Section 7, I mentioned the writer who cut out pictures of people who suggested possible characters to him. Sometimes these were people in the news and sometimes they were faces clipped from advertisements. He pasted them in his idea notebook.

Your idea notebook should be one of your practical working tools and it should also be a source of inspiration to you.

15. HOW WILL A TAPE RECORDER HELP ME?

Since plays are meant to be spoken, it will help you to *hear* your dialogue instead of just reading it. Record it, play it back — not just once but several times so that you really hear all its possible implications and nuances.

When you can, get another person or other people to read the lines for you. This will help you take an objective view of your play and your characters.

Listen to the meaning and the possible inflections in the parts. Does your dialogue reveal what it should? Does it sound realistic or is it stiff? Are the pauses in the right places? Do you need to add pauses or other directions to make the dialogue more meaningful and natural?

Incidentally, when you are recording, don't be afraid to let yourself go. Don't be self-conscious! Put yourself wholeheartedly into the part or parts you are reading. Remember that at this point you are like a detective who is searching for clues. What you are looking for are ways in which you can make your play the best one you have ever written.

16. HOW DO I MAKE A MODEL STAGE?

Your model stage may be as simple or as elaborate as you wish it to be. Keep in mind, however, that what you are making is a tool to help you in writing plays and not a toy or something to be admired by others as an objet d'art.

You can make your stage out of heavy cardboard or wood. The size is again your decision. Pick a size that will be easy for you to work with and one that you have a place for. You will want to have your stage in view and easily accessible to you when you are working on a play.

The model stage size that I have found the most convenient to use is one that has a back and short sides. It is 20 inches wide, 12 inches high, and 10 inches deep.

Your basic model stage need only be a flat piece of wood or heavy cardboard. However, you may find it more helpful to have some sides and a back if you are planning for the traditional stage. A round piece of board will help you plan a play that you want to see presented in a theater-in-the-round setting.

Another type of model theater that you can make has the stage of wood and cardboard sides and back with the necessary doors, windows and fixtures drawn or painted on the cardboard.

It is easy to find furnishings and other materials for your model stage. The average doll house furniture will do nicely. You can get doll house equipment at your local variety store, hobby or toy shop.

Since what you are looking for is a device to help you work out stage movement and other problems, the figures you use for characters can be anything which you can move about.

It is not east to get a set of doll figures to scale that will fit your stage and its furniture. I have seen some sets but they are imported and rather expensive. I suggest instead that you get a package of the inexpensive plastic soldiers that are found in every store that carries toys. They are sturdy and easy to move about. They also come in a variety of positions so that you can have figures standing, sitting or lying down. If you want to distinguish between male and female characters, you can fasten a piece of cloth around those figures which are meant to represent the women in your play.

You can also use the bride and groom figures which can be purchased at gift wrapping counters, or you can make your own stage figures. I know one man who made his out of clothespins, modeling clay and bits of cloth.

A word of warning — small children and kittens are fascinated by the model stage, so if you have either or both in your home, you will want to keep your stage out of small hands' or paws' reach. You may need to make some kind of a transparent cover for your stage.

17. WHAT IS THE PURPOSE OF A MODEL STAGE?

A model stage will help you work out your stage action and directions. By planning your set in miniature, you will be able to see whether or not it is going to be feasible for good performing. For example, in one play, I had arranged the furniture in a way that meant one of the actors would be partially hidden during his speeches. Going through the placement of furniture and the action on the model stage showed that defect very quickly.

By moving your characters about the model stage, you will avoid the problem of having two people in the same place at the same time or by having them too far apart to suit the purposes of their speeches.

A model stage can also serve as an idea stimulator. I once set up one of my model stages with only a chair on it. I kept this stage in view in my office and little by little added other things until I had the setting and the *idea* for a new one-act play.

When you are in the process of writing a play, I suggest that you set up your model stage for that play as simply or as complex as you wish. And keep that stage up-to-date. That is, when you have finished with a section of the play, work it out on the model stage and leave your stage at the point where you have left the manuscript. This will help your to quickly resume writing on the play.

18. HOW MUCH STAGE DIRECTION DO I NEED TO GIVE?

You will need to give all of the entrance and exit cues. You will also give the directions that indicate where a character is when he is on stage and what he is doing. You will also want to indicate certain emotional reactions, such as crying, shouting, laughing, and screaming, as well as the quieter ones like smiling and frowning.

Gestures should be indicated when they have a particular bearing on the action of the play. You will indicate when a character hands something to another character, for instance, if that is relevant to the play's movement. You will want to indicate pauses in the dialogue.

When your play is performed, you will find that both the director and the actors have included bits of stage business of their own. These are meant to add depth to the characterizations, or perhaps lend emphasis to the action of the play. Each actor brings something unique to his part and this you can not write into your play. With your stage directions you are only giving certain basic directions and hints for character development. The more accomplished and professional the actor, the more completely he will be able to develop the part he has been asked to play.

Stage directions are given according to the actor's right or left as he faces the audience. The area near the footlights is downstage and the area toward the back is upstage. Basically, the stage is divided vertically into right, center and left, and horizontally into downstage and upstage. The simplest diagram of this shows 6 stage areas, but you may divide a stage into 8 or 9 areas by subdividing the basic 6 so that you have down right, down center right, down center left, down left, etc. For most purposes the 6 division stage plan will be sufficient.

UR	C	UL
DR	C	DL

——————— AUDIENCE ———————

Here is a sample script with stage directions:
> MARIO (Enters UR)
>> Has anyone here seen tonight's paper?
> LISA (Waving newspaper)
>> I have and I think it's disgraceful
> PHILIP (Moving to her side)
>> And I must say that I agree!
> MARIO (Moving to fireplace)
>> And just what do you intend to do about it?
> PHILIP
>> Well, I (Pause) I guess I really don't know...
> MARIO (laughs scornfully)
>> I didn't thing you'd know what to do!

19. HOW DO I DESCRIBE A STAGE SETTING?

You should describe the stage setting for your play as completely as is needed to visualize your setting. Your description will also help the stage designer and the director plan their work. Don't be too surprised though when a designer sees your setting in a slightly different way than you do. Don't be upset by this! Remember that Shakespeare is played in hundreds of different settings. As he said, "The play's the thing" and your play, if good, can not be harmed by the stage setting. You may not agree with the interpretation by a stage designer but, on the other hand, he may see something in your play that you are blind to because you are its creator.

In describing the stage setting you want to give the physical background for the play. You will tell where the play is taking place and what scenery and furnishings are visible when the curtain rises. For example:

Scene Two, ACT TWO
> The office-laboratory of Mario Martin. Down right is a desk covered with papers and books. It has a telephone, typewriter and radio on it also. Down left is a long table on which there are more papers, jars, bottles and other laboratory equipment. Up center is a kind of machine that looks like an electric water-pump — it has hoses and pipes coming out of it and lying across the floor. Scattered about the room are books, other papers and various pieces of mechanical equipment and tools. There is a door down left.

AT RISE: Mario is seated at his desk, talking on the telephone. The door opens, Lisa rushes in and throws her arms around Mario causing him to drop the telephone.

20. HOW MUCH DO I NEED TO KNOW ABOUT STAGE LIGHTING?

You do not need to be an expert on stage lighting. You should know, however, some fundamental principles of lighting. You can learn all that you need to know by reading a text for drama students. In addition, you can learn a great deal by talking to a stage electrician. Knowing what can and can not be done with lights may influence you in where and how you place your stage furniture and your actors.

21. **WHAT IS A PROPERTY PLOT AND HOW DO I MAKE ONE?**

A property plot is a listing of all the articles, furniture and other things that are used in the play. For example:

                    Property Plot — Act Two
- Desk
- Typewriter
- Telephone
- Radio
- Papers
- Books
- Long table
- Jars, bottles
- Laboratory equipment
- Machine (such as a water pump)
- Hoses and pipes
- Assorted tools

22. **WHAT IS A COSTUME PLOT AND HOW DO I MAKE ONE?**

A costume plot is sometimes combined with the description of the characters. It lists the way in which you see the actors and actresses dressed. For example:

      MARIO MARTIN — Inventor in his 30's
- Sports shirt
- Blue slacks
- Black shoes

You may decide to include just a description of the various characters. This is then usually confined to their basic physical features with some suggestion as to their attitudes and temperament. As:

MARIO MARTIN — In his thirties, tall, attractive and very excitable. He is an inventor and very brilliant. He always sees the most practical side of life.

23.   **HOW MUCH SHOULD I REVISE?**

As much as is necessary! Professional playwrights continue to revise their plays up to curtain time and afterward if they are not satisfied.

After the first writing and verbal tryout you will probably make some changes. And, if your play is being produced locally, you may make revisions during rehearsals if the director or actors find things that need to be changed. Or you may want to make some revisions after a local performance and before you send your play out to publishers, producers or an agent.

A play is like an engine and it may need a "tune-up" or minor adjustments before it is working at its best. Don't be afraid to revise. Use your tape recorder to help you get the feel of the dialogue.

If your play goes out and is rejected, take a fresh look at it when it comes back. I don't mean that you have to continually make revisions, but you should be open to possible changes that will make it a better play.

24. HOW SHOULD A PLAY BE TYPED?

Type on regular 8½" by 11" white typing paper. Double-space your lines. You may want to triple-space between different speeches.

You can either type the names of the characters who are speaking in capital letters at the left of the paper and their dialogue immediately following or on the line below. Another way is to type the names of the characters in capital letters in the center of the page with the dialogue beginning on the next line. For example:

MARIO

I was only concerned with my invention. (Pause) I did not think of the possible consequences, the economic consequences, that is.

LEON

You will save the world but ruin the people. What is the point of it?

Or:

MARIO I was only concerned with my invention. (Pause) I did not think of the possible consequences, the economic consequences, that is.

LEON You will save the world but ruin the people. What is the point of it?

Or:

MARIO

I was only concerned...

Stage directions are given in parentheses after the character's name. Longer, more involved directions are given in parentheses in a separate paragraph.

MARIO (Points to the machine) It was to be a new dawn.

LEON (Taking a gun out of his pocket) It is the setting of the sun, not the rising. (He aims gun at the machine)

(Mario jumps up, runs to Leon and grabs at his arm. They grapple and fall to the floor, rolling over and over.)

25. I HAVE FINISHED MY PLAY; NOW WHAT DO I DO?

Congratulations! You have carried your idea through from its nebulous beginnings to a concrete ending. You now have a finished play!

May I suggest that, before you send it away or take it to some professional or amateur group, you have a kind of private preview for yourself? This is a chance to get rid of any little "bugs" you may have overlooked in the writing.

If your family is interested in your play or you have some interested friends, ask them to help you have a reading of your new work. If you have a large number of characters, some people may have to read more than one part. Get as many copies Xeroxed as you have people taking part. Get together in an evening and read the play aloud. You will find that most people really enjoy doing this. It lets them in on a creative process but it doesn't require acting ability. You may be surprised at how your "actors" will enter into the play just through reading their parts.

Before you start the play, read a brief synopsis so your friends have some idea of what it is all about. Describe the characters to them or have each person read the description of the character or characters he or she is to "play."

You might find it helpful to have a tape recorder going during the session. Listen to it later when you may want to make some revisions based on this first "performance."

During the reading, note where humor shows up. Is it in the lines you thought were funny or is it brought out in other lines? Notice also how the readers tend to accent certain words or speeches. After the reading, don't be afraid to ask why a person interpreted his role as he did.

Invite the participants to give their honest opinions and suggestions after the reading. Ask them if all the motives and actions were clearly stated and understood. At this point, suggestions can be very helpful to you.

You may or may not agree with what is said, but if there are some questions raised about action, characterization or dialogue, you should try to follow through and make revisions if necessary.

When this is all done, then you are ready to send your play out into the world. For information on preparation and mailing, see No. 30.

26. WHY DO I NEED A FINAL SYNOPSIS AFTER THE PLAY IS FINISHED?

Your final synopsis is not a working tool for you but a selling tool. After you have finished your play, make a final, detailed synopsis. This is what you will send as a query to agents or to producers and publishers who want to see a synopsis first. You will also send a copy with your play when you send it out. This helps the producer or the editor decide whether or not he wants to read and consider your play for publication or production.

A producer, an editor, an agent or a publisher receives literally hundreds of play manuscripts. A good synopsis helps him and acts as a salesman for you.

27. CAN I REALLY SELL MY PLAYS?

Yes, you have a chance and should try. Some publishers buy plays and give either royalty payments or a one-time payment. Some periodicals buy plays. Some theater groups pay a royalty fee for each performance.

In addition to royalties and other payments, there are many groups that offer cash prizes for the best plays on certain subjects or the best play written for a specific age group.

28. DO I NEED AN AGENT?

You do need an agent for television (SEE No. 39) but you can manage on your own, without an agent, for plays. In any case, an agent won't be interested in you until you have established some kind of production record.

You can find lists of agents and their requirements in *The Writer's Market* and similar books. When writing a query to an agent, be sure and send any copies of reviews of plays that you have had produced and send a list of where your plays have been produced and/or published.

29. WHERE CAN I FIND PLACES TO SEND MY PLAYS?

There are lists of places which want to see plays whether for publication or for production. The best sources for that information are monthly writers' magazines and various yearbooks. The two magazines are: *The Writer,* and *Writer's Digest.*

Each year in an issue of *The Writer* there is a special market list devoted to drama markets which includes market lists for radio and television as well as the stage. This list also gives the necessary information about play publishers and magazines interested in publishing plays. In addition, there is an up-to-date list of regional and university theaters that are interested in seeing scripts.

You should, if you can, subscribe to these magazines, as all through the year they have information that will be of interest to you as a playwright. They are excellent sources of news about current contests and awards for plays. During the year, they will also have articles on drama by well-known playwrights and others connected with the theater.

Most public and college libraries subscribe to *The Writer* and *Writer's Digest* so that they are readily accessible. Issues are also found at newsstands and stores where magazines are sold.

Writer's Market is an annual publication. It contains a list of play producers, play publishers, agents and all kinds of facts related to writing. It is a highly useful book and can be purchased at your local bookstore or ordered directly from the publisher. The address is the same as that given above for the magazine *Writer's Digest.*

It will be up to you to keep abreast of local and regional theater possibilities in your own area. Newspapers are the best source for this information.

When selecting a place to send your play, be sure that you read the market requirements very carefully. For example, some publishers or producers want only one-act plays. Some other places will not look at a script unless it has already been tried out on the stage in local production.

30. HOW SHOULD I PREPARE MY MANUSCRIPT FOR MAILING?

When you have decided that your play is ready for submission and it has been properly typed and you have decided where you are going to send it, you are ready to mail it out.

A short play may be sent in a large manila envelope. A long play may be sent in a Jiffy bag or in a box in which typing paper is sold.

As a rule, I would send a play loose to publishers, but in a folder or binder to a producer.

Although you can mail manuscripts at a special rate by marking them SPECIAL FOURTH CLASS RATE — MANUSCRIPT, I think that it is worth the extra money to send them by first-class mail. The special fourth class rate can only be used for mail within the U.S. If your manuscript weighs under one pound, it is just as economical to use first class.

Be sure to enclose a self-addressed envelope with return postage or, if using a Jiffy bag or box, enclose return postage and a return label.

31. WHAT INFORMATION SHOULD I SEND ALONG WITH THE SUBMITTED PLAY?

It is helpful to send a synopsis. You should also send a letter telling something about your background in dramatics. If the play you are sending has been produced anywhere, include Xerox copies of the programs and any newspaper reviews. If you have had other plays produced and reviewed, send copies of those reviews.

32. WHAT KIND OF RECORDS SHOULD I KEEP?

When you have just one play in your file, there is no problem with knowing where it is, where it has been produced and who has looked at it. But when you have two, then three and more and more plays (as I hope you will), then you have to rely on records rather than your memory.

You will want to have a file card for each play. I suggest using 5" × 8" cards. Have a file box for the cards, either of metal or of heavy cardboard, and alphabet guide cards.

On the card put the name of the play, number of acts and scenes, number of characters and number of sets. Below this information, list the places where you have sent the play, the action taken, where it has been performed and any other pertinent information.

Your card will look something like this:

The Glass Beehive   3 acts, 2 scenes   8 chars. (5m, 3f)   2 sets

Date	To	Action
2/7/83	Central College Drama Dept.	Not at this time
4/10/83	College Club Play Group	Read at meeting on 5/6/83
5/15/83	Central City Community Theater	Produced — 6 performances at McMillan School Auditorium 7/5/83 - 7/10/83
10/6/83	Central College Drama Dept.	Produced — 3 performances at Cornell Auditorium 11/23/83 - 11/25/83
12/31/83	Samuel French	

When you write a great many plays, you will probably find it useful to have a character file. This can be kept on 3" × 5" cards in a file case. On each card give the name of the character, the play in which he appears and a brief description. A card might look like this:

    Martin, Mario   *The Glass Beehive*
    Inventor of anti-pollution device.
    In his 30's.

You will also want to keep a scrapbook of any reviews you get when your plays are produced.

33. WHAT ABOUT PLAY PRODUCTION?

Plays are written to be produced on the stage or on the screen. Every playwright, in his own mind, visualizes the production of his brain child. At the same time he fears what others — producers, directors, stage designers, and actors — may do to his creation. The playwright imagines the ideal production, but more often than not, "real life" comes up with another production which is more feasible and more economical.

When your play is ready for production and, hopefully, you have found an interested group, you have to let go a little and let the others move in and work their own miracles.

If possible, you should work with them but not in a temperamental way. By working with the director, costumers, designers and actors, you can discover what is right and what is wrong with your play. Rehearsals may often dismay you, but they will show you the weak and strong spots in your play.

What should you do when you are asked to rewrite? As a rule, I would follow the suggestions of the director and the actors. They are the ones who are doing it. They are the ones who are responsible for bringing your play to life. Ask them why they feel a certain scene has to be rewritten or a scene omitted, line deleted, etc. Try to be impartial. Don't be afraid to argue your viewpoint and give your own reasons, but don't be stubborn about it.

A play may look great on paper but the true test comes when it is acted out by real people on a stage. Major or minor flaws will show up. Unless corrected, these flaws will impede the play's action, change the meaning and probably lose the audience.

Be grateful for production. It is the real test of the validity of your play.

34. HOW CAN I GET MY PLAYS PERFORMED?

Having written your play and satisfied yourself that it is now finally finished and ready for production, your next step is to find a stage company.

Locally you should contact your amateur theater group. In some towns there are several groups that are interested in putting on plays and that are usually at least willing to look at a script by an unknown and a local plawright. You may be fortunate enough to live in a town where there are semi-professional or professional theater groups. Get in touch with the directors of such companies. Let them have a synopsis and a script to look at. Always indicate your willingness to work with them on any requested changes.

College and high school dramatic groups offer other production possibilities. Get in touch with the dramatics or play production teacher.

If your town has no dramatic group, you might want to start one yourself. As a playwright, you have a definite interest and stake in regional theater. Your chances of getting your play produced on Broadway are slight, but you do have more opportunity to get your play performed locally and regionally. Who knows, then, where a good play could go! By being realistic in your approach to production, you will not only avoid disappointment, but also you will stand a better chance of seeing some of your plays being acted.

Don't overlook church dramatic groups. They are doing some interesting and exciting things. Another advantage is that a church social hall often has all the facilities needed to put on a play — from a stage, to chairs for the audience. And, since the first dramatic performances were connected with religious rites, a church setting does not seem too inappropriate.

A word of caution — be sure that the subject matter of your play is suited for the dramatic group to which you are offering it. Keep in mind the range of capabilities of the group members and their own subject interests. It should be obvious that some subjects might be taboo for high school or church groups.

35. WON'T AMATEURS RUIN MY PLAY?

Just like playwrights, amateur actors vary in degree of excellence and capability. A good play may not be enhanced by poor acting, but it can not be totally destroyed. On the other hand, the best actors in the world can not save a badly written play.

Most amateur acting groups are very dedicated and sincere. A playwright can learn a great deal from seeing his work in production. If it does not come off well in the amateur theater, be sure you examine your play before blaming the actors.

36. SHOULD I DIRECT OR ACT IN MY OWN PLAYS?

The answer to this question really lies in the answer to two other questions: 1. Can you direct? and 2. Can you act? If you can do one or both, then why not? However, a word of caution: The playwright sees things one way, the director another way and the actor may have still other notions. Can you be at war with yourself if necessary?

Also, can you be impartial enough to see weak spots or other character interpretations that might not fit in with your own preconceived ideas? You should be very sure of your ability to be so versatile before you attempt to run the whole show by yourself.

37. WHAT ABOUT HAVING PLAYS PUBLISHED?

There are publishers and periodicals that publish plays. The competition is very great but you should try. Information on where to send is found in writing magazines and books (SEE Section 29 and Bibliography). Some publishers pay royalties and some buy outright. In any case, until you are well-known, the money involved is not likely to be too much. It's always a thrill, though, to see your name and your play in print. And publication adds to your credits when you submit other plays to producers or publishers.

38. NO ONE SEEMS INTERESTED IN MY PLAYS — WHAT SHOULD I DO NOW?

Are you sure that you have tried all kinds of outlets for your plays? It is easy to get discouraged, but never allow disappointment to take over your thinking.

If you have tried all possibilites and can not get any form of encouragement, you will have to decide if you are satisfied to just write plays for your own amusement. There's nothing wrong in doing that, but it may not be the only answer. Maybe you should be writing something else.

Take one of your play plots and put it into a different literary form, such as a story or novel. How does it work? How do you enjoy writing in this form? What kind of a reponse do you get from others when they read it? The answers to these questions will tell you if you were perhaps mistaken in writing plays.

If your interest in writing plays is really an interest in theater, perhaps you should become involved in some other aspect of the theater — acting, directing, designing or stage management.

If your plots seem good but the problem lies in your dialogue or action, see if you can find another writer who is strong in the areas where you are weak and who would like to collaborate with you. Better to be a joint author than no author at all!

39. WHAT ABOUT WRITING FOR TELEVISION?

Television, because of its popularity and ubiquitous presence, seems like the ideal place for scripts. It is and it isn't. It *is* because it requires, like a hungry monster, a lot of material. It *isn't* because the beginner does not have much chance.

Television scripts are usually only bought through agents. Very few agents will look at material submitted by an unknown writer, however, some of them will look at query letters.

You can find a list of agents and what their requirements are in the *Writer's Market, The Writer's Handbook,* and books directed specifically to television script writers.

The preparation of a television script is different from that of a play script. To become familiar with television script requirements, read some of the books which are now on the market for the beginning television writer.

And, of course, you will have to allow some time for watching television so that you will know what shows are popular and what themes are "in" for the season. Keep in mind, though, that television is a fickle medium and cycles come to an end. If you have an original concept, you might be the one to start a whole new trend.

Some television shows are willing to look at scripts from outside writers. Television market lists will tell you which ones to contact. Be very familiar with the program, its characters and theme line before attempting to submit a script.

Don't overlook the educational, industrial and business audiovisual fields.

40. WHAT ABOUT WRITING FOR THE MOVIES?

Most of what is said in Section 39 also applies to writing for the movies. Again it is difficult to sell a script without an agent.

Script writing for the movies also has some definite requirements and limitations. The best way to become familiar with those special needs is to study sample scripts and directions in a book on screenwriting. (See Bibliography)

41. I CAN'T FINISH MY PLAY: WHAT CAN I DO TO GET GOING AGAIN?

So you've started a play, perhaps even completed most of it, and suddenly you seem to have come to a dead end! Don't be alarmed — it happens to the best writers at times.

There are a number of things which you can do. One is to put the play away and stop consciously thinking about it. Relax and put it out of your mind. Get involved in a hobby, go out to dinner, visit friends, read a book or watch television. You may find that you will come up with a solution to your dramatic problem or end your writer's block quite easily and naturally. This is because while you have put it out of your conscious mind, your unconscious still has it very much in focus. You have been trying too hard and actually blocking your own thought processes.

Even if no ideas come to you, you will find that when you return to your play after a period of relaxation, you will be able to write again and that the ideas will come to you.

Your idea notebook is a great help when you are stymied in a play. Going through your notes may either give you what you need or trigger a suggestion that will help you.

Also, take a closer look at your play. Perhaps you are trying to make a three-act play out of a one-act or two-act play. You may have become stuck just because there really isn't anything more to say!

Take a short story or a novel and see if you can make a play out of it. This can be a good stimulus for you. Of course, if you were to put it on the stage, you would have to get permission form the original author and his publisher.

42. DO YOU HAVE ANY FINAL WORDS OF ADVICE?

Yes. Don't get discouraged! Keep on writing plays if you are convinced that drama is the right form for your creative talents. Make your writing a part of your regular life routines. Above all, get enjoyment from what you write, but always keep good craftsmanship firmly in mind.

LOCAL HISTORY

At a time when the world seems so much involved in global problems and space exploration, some might question the role and importance of local history. But local history is the true beginnings of all history. Local history is a microcosm of the larger scene. It is the true story of the individuals who together make up the whole community of man.

Local history is a record of many small dreams, but those dreams are backed by the same enthusiasm and perseverance that send men out on the larger adventures.

1. WHAT IS LOCAL HISTORY?

Local history is the history of people, events and institutions in a specifically designated and geographically circumscribed area.

2. IS LOCAL HISTORY ENTIRELY INDEPENDENT OF NATIONAL OR INTERNATIONAL HISTORY?

No, because no place can be totally isolated. The events of the larger scene do and always have affected the local scene. The difference today is that with the speed and ease of modern communications, national conditions and events are felt almost instantaneously at the local level as well. But all through history, wars, revolutions, new inventions and current economic conditions have had their effects upon the local scene.

Yes, local history is specialized, but it is directly related to and influenced by what happens in the world outside.

3. WHY COLLECT AND WRITE LOCAL HISTORY?

Local history should be collected and preserved because it is an essential part of the national heritage.

In *War and Peace*, Tolstoy wrote: "The subject of history is the life of peoples and of humanity." Local history is the account of the everyday lives of peoples, their dreams, their aspirations and their achievements.

The journey to the moon was probably the greatest achievement of this century but this should not blind us to the daily record of human concerns. A centennial celebration in a small Western town does not get the publicity that a moon shot does but for that area it is a more relevant and important event. And, it should be documented in pictures and writing because it, along with thousands of other community events, makes up the totality of our national history.

4. DO YOU HAVE TO BE A PROFESSIONAL HISTORIAN TO WRITE LOCAL HISTORY?

No. In fact it is a rare community that has a professional historian ready and willing to write about it. Most local history is written by amateurs. The amateur historian brings to his work an enthusiastic zeal and a love for his subject that often transcends any minor flaws in writing.

The amateur historian can be and usually is as well trained in basic methods as the professional historian. The difference between them should be in the scope of the subject covered and the depth, not the competency of the work itself.

5. WHAT SPECIAL APTITUDES SHOULD THE WRITER OF LOCAL HISTORY HAVE?

He or she should first of all be trememdously interested in and excited about the subject. He should be willing to spend hours in research if necessary. (Some research may become tedious at times.)

He must have a detective's mind, for much history, especially local history, has to be uncovered from hints, from footnotes and from chance remarks and encounters.

A local historian must know his area and the people of his area. He has to be tactful when dealing with people, particulary with people who may hold opposing views of a local historical personage or event.

He has to have patience because collecting and writing local history takes not only tact but time.

6. IS LOCAL HISTORY SALABLE?

Yes. True, your market is limited as a rule. Local history is of interest in a rather narrow geographical area. You can, however, find markets in your regional area.

This does not mean that you may not be able to sell to a wider market. There are national publications which take articles of interest on local subjects. Keep in mind that you will have to write about a subject that would interest readers who do not live in the immediate area.

7. WHAT ARE SOME OF THE MARKET POSSIBILITES FOR LOCAL HISTORY?

First of all, there are your local and regional newspapers. If you live in or near a large city, the Sunday edition of the paper often has a special supplement which uses feature articles, particulary about local history.

Check on the regional magazines. They are often in the market for local history stories.

If you have a local history story that you feel would be of interest to a wider audience, consult the special publications that are issued for writers. There are monthly magazines and annual yearbooks.

Writer's Market and *Writer's Yearbook* and *The Writer's Handbook* are three very useful annual publications. For example, *Writer's Market* lists history magazines and their requirements.

Two invaluable monthly magazines are *The Writer* and *Writer's Digest* These give market listings, writing tips and informative and helpful articles on all phases of writing.

Most public libraries have the publications mentioned above or you may get them directly from the publishers.

8. WHAT ARE SOME OF THE PUBLIC SOURCES OF LOCAL HISTORY?

The availablility of local history source material is to some extent dependent upon your location. If you live in an area which has produced a native son or daughter who went on to become a person of national importance, you will find that more has been written about your area and that person. If you are in an area which as been the scene of some national event, such as a Civil or Revolutionary War battle, there is practically no end to what is available. A region which abounds in natural wonders has also no doubt attracted much attention already. However, do not feel discouraged for the history of a lesser known place is just as important although perhaps not as easy to track down.

Here is a list of some of the public sources of history:

    Tax records.
    Telephone books.
    City directories.
    Local and regional maps.
    Census reports.
    Voter lists.
    Abstracts of property titles.
    School records.
    Council and Commission minutes.
    City, county and village histories.
    State and regional histories.
    Anniversary booklets.
    Company histories.
    Club yearbooks.
    School annuals.
    Local newspapers and magazines.
    Regional newspapers and magazines.

You may find only a sentence or two in each book if you are working on a special topic, but taken altogether, these sources can provide you with much useful information.

Many early histories — especially county, city and village histories — were commercial ventures in which emphasis was placed upon leading citizens and their activities. The financing of these books was often done by the individuals who were mentioned in the text. Although some of the facts may not be accurate, these books (which usually contain portraits) are a prime source of local history.

Some early histories were written under the auspices of the local historical society or a local club. Most of these, while small in number of pages, contain information that may not be available in any other publication.

Anniversary booklets and company histories may be suspect in some of the facts for there is a natural tendency to emphasize the good rather than the bad in such publications. However, these booklets are particularly valuable for their illustrations. Interested citizens often contribute photographs that have never before been published.

In using any of this material it is best to ask yourself what the purpose of the publication was. It is also wise to take into account who (whether a person or a group of people) was responsible for the material. This will help you decide on the best use you can make of that material.

9. WHAT ARE SOME OF THE PRIVATE SOURCES OF LOCAL HISTORY?

Private sources of local history are as varied as the public sources. They are often not as obvious and sometimes ferreting them out requires quite a bit of detective work on your part.

Here is a list of some possible private sources:

        Account books.
        Family albums.
        Diaries and journals.
        Letters.
        Genealogies.
        Scrapbooks.
        Business ledgers and correspondence.

You may come across account books that have been kept by individuals as well as by business firms. Account books can tell you a lot about the economic life of a community.

Business account books will have a record of prices, kinds of merchandise and the names of customers.

Private account books will give you a picture of how the ordinary person spent his or her money. It will list for you both the necessities and luxuries of life during a specific time period.

Family albums provide a pictorial record of both a people and a locality. There are usually photographs of special civic events such as parades or community celebratons. In albums, you can see what people wore and what they did for amusement. An album can also accurately depict the common architectural designs and changes in an area.

When studying and using family albums, don't forget to pay attention to the background in the pictures. While capturing the image of the person may have been the photographer's intent, you can pick up useful information about a period or place by noting the furnishings, the buildings or locale in the picture.

Diaries and journals are basic tools of local history research. They offer comments on daily life, common concerns, world events especially as they relate to local affairs, economic problems, religious and social controversies and area customs. Depending of course upon the education, the interests and age of the writer, diaries and journals will vary in colorfulness as well as in accuracy.

Letters are perhaps the most intimate of the private sources of local history. Like diaries, letters give a very personal view of private and public affairs. Letters are often painfully truthful regarding events and interpersonal relationships.

Genealogies tell you who is related to whom and often where people were at particular times. Some genealogies will also include fragments of community history.

Scrapbooks are a good source of information about how the individual and the community were interrelated. Many scrapbooks also contain pictures.

10. HOW DO I GET TO USE THESE VARIOUS SOURCES OF LOCAL HISTORY?

Public sources are easy to get to. They are a matter of public knowledge and accessibility.

To make private sources available for your use, you will have to let people know that you are interested in this material. Get your local paper to run a notice for you. Pass the word around that you are looking for source material for local history. If you have a local history society, join it and work through the society.

Visit the "old-timers" in your town and region. Talk with them. Ask them if they have any letters diaries, albums or similar material that they would let you examine and use. Record their memories. (See Nos. 22 - 28)

Always be careful with the material that is lent to you. Assure individuals that you are aware of your responsibility when you borrow materials.

Go to auctions, garage sales and secondhand stores. You never know when you may find a local history treasure.

11. WHAT IS THE BEST SOURCE OF LOCAL HISTORY?

Undoubtedly, the best source of local history is the newspaper. The newpaper is a record of the area, the people, the customes, the economic conditions, the festivities and the tragedies. It tells what was of current interest and importance at the time that it happened. We should not forget that before television and radio, newspapers were the lifeline of public communication. Even now, when they have to share the spotlight, newspapers continue to be a major source of contemporary local history.

Newspapers not only contain news about current events, people and issues, but their advertisements are a source of historical information. Prices, availability of merchandise, kinds of things that were in demand and other important facts may be gleaned from the advertisements.

Newspapers also print notices of elections, legal announcements, auctions, city ordinances and other public announcements.

In using any newspaper as a source for local history, keep in mind that most papers reflect a partisan viewpoint in politics and local events.

12. WHAT ARE THE LEGAL IMPLICATIONS IN USING DIARIES, LETTERS, ETC.?

If you have any doubts about your legal rights to use material from private sources, consult a lawyer. Usually, however, you can draft a simple letter of permission which the owner of the documents can sign. Always be sure that the person concerned knows what you want to do with the material. This is especially important if you are going to publish the material either *in toto* or excerpted.

When letters, diaries or other material affect a family, it is a good idea to be sure that all members of the family agree on whether or not you have the right to use the material.

If an individual or a family requests that you omit certain facts or do not use specific portions, accede to that request.

If persons are still living or descendants of persons are living and there is any question about material being libellous or derogatory, don't publish it. Unless, of course, they themselves insist that you put historical accuracy before the family name!

Material which you collect can always be preserved by your historical society or library if you feel you can not safely publish it at the time.

13. CAN I REPRINT MATERIAL FROM EARLIER PUBLISHED SOURCES?

Yes, if such material is now in the public domain. That is, if it is no longer under copyright. Copyright information is given in each book or periodical. You should, however, always note the original publication, giving full bibliographical details.

14. CAN I QUOTE FROM CONTEMPORARY SOURCES?

You can only quote from copyrighted material in an amount that would not be considered an infringement upon the copyright. Since it is sometimes difficult to tell just what constitutes infringement, it is safer to write to the publisher for permission if you intend to quote more than a line or two.

Most publishers are happy to give you permission to reprint excerpts provided you acknowledge the original source in your book.

15. SHOULD I PUBLISH MY OWN BOOK ON LOCAL HISTORY?

Yes, if you want to invest your time and money in that project. Local history does have a market. Area residents, bookstores and libraries will usually purchase books on local history.

Keep your limited market in mind when ordering the number of copies you want printed. It is better and more satisfying to sell out your edition than to have boxes of unsold books around the house or stored in the garage. If you have a "best seller" and there is a continuing demand, you can always reprint your book.

Another solution to publishing your material is to work on a cooperative basis with an historical society, newspaper, museum or printer. In this way you can share the costs and later the profits.

16. HOW WILL LEARNING TO USE A CAMERA HELP ME?

Local history is more than a written record — it is also a pictorial record. And, local history is not just the ancient past — it is also the present and those remnants of yesterday that still exist.

Photographing buildings, specific areas, individuals and events is a continuing part of your local history research. You can use photographs to enhance your history text. Or, you may want to do a local history story in which the photographs are the most important part.

With today's cameras you do not have to be a professional photographer to get good pictures. If you follow the manufacturer's directions, you should get photographs that are usable. There are also a number of good photography books that can help you get the most out ot the equipment that you have.

If, despite your best efforts, you can not learn to take pictures, make friends with a person who can take pictures and who shares your interest in preserving local history.

Whether you take the pictures yourself or someone else does, be sure that each photograph is carefully and accurately documented. Know where a picture was taken, the date and the names of any persons or buildings in that picture. While you know what or who you were photographing at the time, it is very hard to recall the facts a few months later.

17. WHEN SHOULD I USE OLD PHOTOGRAPHS?

Use old photographs whenever it is pertinent to your text. For example, you may want to use an old photograph showing how Main St. looked in 1890 as contrasted with a modern photograph showing how it looks today.
Early photographs of people, places and events all add to your written historical account. Readers like to see for themselves "how it was."

18. WHERE CAN I FIND OLD PHOTOGRAPHS?

There are several sources for old photographs. Local citizens often have photographic albums, pictures of their families, portraits of their grandparents and other relatives, school-related photographs and pictures of spcecial events, especially if they or members of their family were involved in any way.

The local newspaper may have a picture morgue. Check with commercial photographers especially if they have been in business for a long time.

Among the institutions that often have photographic archives are state and local historical societies, museums, state, public and college libraries. In some of the larger institutions there may be a photo historian who will be able to give you help and advice. When you find photographs that you want, you can usually have copies made for a reasonable fee.

In your book or article you should note the source of photographs you have used. It is also customary to give the individual or institution a copy of the book or article when it is published.

19. WHAT KINDS OF FILES SHOULD I KEEP?

As a writer of local history, you are going to inevitably collect a certain amount of material. Even when you are using library and museum collections, you still will want some material of your own. In addition, you will very rapidly accumulate a pile of notes and other papers from your research.

You should get a file cabinet. Whether you get a two-drawer, or a four- or five-drawer will depend upon how much collecting of material you anticipate doing. Get file folders and a marking pen and arrange your material in the way that is most logical for your own use. Do not worry about whether or not you are doing a professional job of arranging and filing. The whole purpose to this is that you are going to be able to find your material when you need it.

The sophistication of your filing system will have to depend upon the extent of your research. For example, if your local history project is the compilation of material relating to the Fire Department, your files might be like this:

     Duty Rosters
     Equipment
     Finances
     Firehouses
     Founders
     Fund Raising
     Major Fires
     Officers

In a large project, your files would be further subdivided by dates. For instance:

     Duty Rosters   1900-1920
     Duty Rosters   1921-1935

  Notes from books can be kept on file cards. I recommend 5" × 8" cards. These should be kept in a file box. Again, they should be arranged in the way that is most convenient for you, the user. A subject arrangement is usually the most practical. A project on a single historical incident can be arranged by dates.

20. SHOULD I DO MY OWN INDEXING WHEN NO INDEX IS PRINTED OR AVAILABLE?

  Indexing your material will save you hours or time when working on various historical projects. It is very frustrating to have to search through a manuscript or a printed volume in search of a fact, a name or a date.

  For example, if you have a printed volume which contains local history but has no index, your first job in using that book will be to prepare your own index. Using file cards (3" × 4" or 5" × 8") go through the book page by page and note all information with the page on which it is located. In particular, you will want to note personal names, place-names, important dates and events.

  Some of your cards might look like this:

     SMITH, ROGER ADAMS
     Elected mayor — p. 31
     Founded First National Bank — p. 104
     Medal of Honor — P. 210
     Died — p. 250
             SHWC

     OLDHAM BRIDGE
     First proposed — p. 5
     Funds — p. 7
     Competition for design — p. 15
     Dedication — p. 21
     Wilderness River Floor — p. 125
     Replacement — p. 133
             SHWC

  Be sure that each card carries the notation of the book or manuscript which is being indexed. In the example above, the letters SHWC stand for *Sander's*

History of Washington County.

The same indexing procedure should be followed with unindexed manuscripts, letters and periodicals that you use regularly in your research.

21. WHAT ARE SOME OTHER SPECIALIZED SOURCES OF LOCAL HISTORY?

There are some other sources of local history which are different from those which we usually associate with the subject. More closely allied with oral history, these sources are a product of our new technology.

Most radio stations make tapes of their broadcasts, especially of programs that contain interviews with local persons. Many stations have regularly scheduled programs that feature information about events, special community celebrations and interviews with visiting and local celebrities.
Television stations may also have video tape that has local events, individuals and news featured.

22. WHAT IS ORAL HISTORY?

Oral history is the recording of spoken history, usually reminiscences. It is recorded on tape, reel or cassette or sometimes on video tape which combines the visual with the oral. The subject matter may vary but it all concerns some aspect of local history. The people being interviewed need not be persons of fame and importance. In fact, lesser-known individuals often have more material of value to contribute, material related to how everyday life was lived. These recollections and observations form a cornerstone for local history.

23. WHAT PREPARATIONS SHOULD BE MADE FOR THE ORAL HISTORY INTERVIEW?

Select the individuals that you think can contribute to the field and then obtain their consent for interviews. Written consent is essential if you are going to use some of the material in an article or book. It will save time if they know in advance what you are going to talk about. Use some care in selecting people as not every individual is able to automatically provide you with the information you want.

As the interviewer, you should do extensive research on the individual, subject, time period to be covered or event. Take notes. This will help you to check on the accuracy of the interviewee's remarks and enable you to resolve any discrepancies that occur. It will also make you appear to be both knowledgeable and interested, factors which should help put the interviewee at ease.

Check your equipment before going to the interview. Be sure you have everything you need. Unless you know the arrangement of the area where you are doing the interview, it is wise to have a tape recorder that works on either batteries or electricity. I have also found it useful to take a long extension cord as sometimes the nearest outlet is across the room.

24. HOW DO I USE THE TAPE RECORDER WHEN INTERVIEWING?

Many people are nervous and ill at ease when being recorded. The interviewer should, therefore, spend the first few minutes of the session in casual conversation and in explaining the mechanics of the recorder. Some interviewees will want to hold the microphone; others will prefer that it be placed on a table. A brief test for voice level should be made and played back. When the interviewee is relaxed, the interview can begin.

25. HOW STRUCTURED SHOULD THE INTERVIEW BE?

This will depend upon the person being interviewed. Some individuals need a minimum of prompting to start and to continue talking. Others respond best to direct questions. You should be prepared with a list of questions and suggested topics. While it is advisable to keep the interviewee on the subject sometimes digressions can be more interesting and rewarding then the original subject. As the interviewer, you have to use discretion and common sense as to how far afield you can go. Excessive rambling by the interviewee can be tactfully checked by well-timed questions.

26. HOW LONG SHOULD AN ORAL HISTORY SESSION BE?

Usually one hour sessions are the most productive and the number of sessions will depend on the individual and the subject matter. Obviously older people or people in poor health will tire more easily and should not be subjected to long sessions.

If you are recording away from your town, the amount of time scheduled for interviews may be determined by the time you have to spend in that locale.

27. WHAT IS THE NEXT STEP AFTER THE TAPING?

After the interview or series of interviews are completed, you will want to transcribe the tape into manuscript form. It should be written down as it was said on the tape. Obvious errors can be noted in the manuscript copy with the word *sic* in parentheses. As in this statement, "We moved to Elm City in 1992 (sic) and opened our first store at that time." In such cases you should check back with the interviewee and get the correct date which you can then append as a note to the transcription.

In some cases the interviewee may stipulate and insist on the right to check the written transcription.

28. HOW CAN ORAL HISTORY BE USED?

There are many uses for oral history. For the writer and researcher it offers one more excellent source of information — information not usually found in published material. The historian, especially the local historian, can frequently uncover new sources and find personal views of important events. For the fiction or feature writer it presents a wealth of new material usually not available elsewhere. It is especially useful for recording the memoirs of early settlers and local civic and political leaders.

When the interviewer has completed the project, copies of the tapes and/or transcripts may be given to a local library or university for permanent preservation. You will, of course, need the consent of the interviewee and should have this in writing.

29. HOW CAN LOCAL HISTORY BE A COMMUNITY FUND-RAISING PROJECT?

Local history makes an ideal fund-raising project for a community group, service club, church or even the entire town.

Everyone is interested in local history. They want to know about past history. They want a record of the present. Whether it is the history of a region, town, or one single entity of that town, it has readers waiting.

Many community groups have raised money for worthwhile civic projects by books or pamphlets on local history.

It can be both educational and fun to work on a committee that is gathering material for such a local history project. In addition, the sponsoring group has the satisfaction of knowing that they are preserving something which might otherwise be lost.

30. SHOULD THERE BE A LOCAL HISTORY ORGANIZATION?

Yes! As a writer who is interested in local history, you should also be willing to encourage a local history organization. If your community already has such an organization, become an active member. If there is no existing organization, start one!

Your local public library may be willing to assist you in providing a place to meet. If the library does not have a place, the social hall of a local church is another possibility.

No community is too small to have a local historical association. You will enjoy sharing your interests with like-minded persons. In addition, you will have the satisfaction of knowing that you are all working together to preserve the history and heritage of your country and civilization.

31. WHAT ARE MY RESPONSIBILITIES AS A COLLECTOR AND WRITER OF LOCAL HISTORY?

You should collect local history with understanding and wisdom. You should cultivate the arts of observation, perception and good writing. You should combine a love for historical accuracy with a sense of reponsibility for individual privacy.

As a writer and collector you should resist all temptations to hoard your material and information. You should be willing to share what you have discovered with others. Only a small part of your obligation is custodial in nature. Your greater obligation is to disseminate the information you have gathered. You can do this through publication, through lecturing and by letting others use your source materials.

In particular, you should be sure that the children and young people in your town or city are aware of what is being done to collect and preserve local history. They are the future and they need to know about the past. Local history is their history. It can give them a much-needed feeling of belonging to the community.

COPYRIGHT AND CONTRACT

There are two legal items you need to be concerned with — copyright and contracts. Both are connected with your rights and should be properly used so that they protect those rights.

1. **WHERE CAN I GET INFORMATION ON COPYRIGHT LAWS AND PROCEDURES?**

Free circulars and a catalog of books and microfiche on copyright which are for sale are available from the U.S. Copyright Office. There are also articles from time to time in the various writers magazines which offer summaries of copyright law. The free circulars will answer all your basic questions.
Write to: Copyright Office
               Library of Congress
               Washington, D.C. 20559

The Copyright Office does not give legal advice, that you must get from an attorney or legal service.

2. **ACCORDING TO COPYRIGHT LAW, WHAT ARE MY RIGHTS?**

Under the provisions of the new Copyright Act that became law on January 1, 1978, copyright automatically exists from the minute a work is created and fixed in a tangible medium, that is, manuscript, book, film, record, tape, etc. In other words, copyright (your rights) exists once you can read it, see it, or hear it.

3. **HOW LONG DO THOSE RIGHTS BELONG TO ME?**

They are yours for the rest of your life unless you assign them to someone else.

4. **WHAT HAPPENS TO THOSE RIGHTS IF I DIE?**

The rights you had at the time of your death belong to your heirs for fifty years after your death.

5. **IF COPYRIGHT IS AUTOMATIC, WHY SHOULD I REGISTER MY COPYRIGHT?**

Registering your copyright establishes a public record of your claim. It means that you have proof if you need to file an infringement suit at any time.

6. **HOW DO I REGISTER MY WORK?**

You need to send a filled-out application form (use black ink or a typewriter), a filing fee of $10. Do not send cash. You must also include one copy of the work if it is unpublished or two copies if it is published. All of these items must be sent together to the Register of Copyrights, Copyright Office, Library of Congress, Washington, D.C. 20559.

7. HOW DO I KNOW WHAT COPYRIGHT APPLICATION FORM TO USE?

The free pamphlets (see no. 1) will tell you or you can write and ask for the correct form, stating what you want to have copyrighted. For example, Form TX is the form for published and unpublished nondramatic literary works.

8. HOW LONG BEFORE I GET MY COPYRIGHT REGISTRATION BACK?

It can be as long as ninety days, depending upon the volume of work in the Copyright Office. However, your copyright registration takes effect on the date of receipt of your application in the Copyright Office.

9. HOW DO I INDICATE COPYRIGHT ON MY WORK?

The symbol for the word "copyright", the year of first publication and the name of the copyright owner must be in a reasonably conspicuous place. In printed books, it is usually found on the verso of the title page. In unpublished manuscripts it is found on the front pages or title page.
Examples: © 1984 Mary Lee Smith
Copyright © 1984 The Handsel Foundation
Unpublished work © 1984 Ben Davies

10. MY PUBLISHER SAYS HE WILL TAKE CARE OF THE COPYRIGHT REGISTRATION, IS THAT ALL RIGHT?

Yes, most publishers do this as a service to their authors. They send in the application form, fee and copies of the printed book. Your contract should specify and it be understood by both parties how the copyright is to be registered. It is customary to have it in the author's name unless the book was done for hire and it is considered to be the property of the publisher or some other agency.

11. CAN I GET AN INTERNATIONAL COPYRIGHT?

No, there is no international copyright. The United States is a member of the Universal Copyright Convention (the UCC) and in general, all the countries that belong respect the copyrights taken out in member countries. However, some countries do not offer copyright protection for foreign works.

12. WHAT ITEMS SHOULD I BE SURE ARE COVERED IN MY CONTRACT?

When your manuscript is to be delivered.
How many copies of the manuscript you are to provide.
What rights are being assigned or sold.

The royalty percentage and when royalties are to be paid.
When the book is to be published.
There are some other details but they are covered in the sections below.

13. IF I DON'T LIKE SOME OF THE PROVISIONS IN MY CONTRACT, CAN I GET THE PUBLISHER TO CHANGE THEM?

If you are unhappy with any of the sections of your contract, you should certainly talk it over with your publisher. If you have a good and valid reason for asking for a change, the publisher may agree. On the other hand, you will often find that the publisher has valid reasons for the provisions of the contract that relate to production, distribution and other concerns of publishing.

Any changes that are made should be initialed by you and the responsible representative of the publisher.

14. I'M NOT SURE I UNDERSTAND MY CONTRACT, WHAT SHOULD I DO?

First, ask your publisher to explain the contract to you. If you still have questions or feel uneasy about any portion of the contract, go to a lawyer. Don't sign any contract while you have questions about it.

15. MY CONTRACT STATES MY MANUSCRIPT IS TO BE HANDED IN BY A CERTAIN DATE BUT WHAT IF I CAN'T FINISH IT BY THEN?

If you think you are going to be late, notify your publisher at once. Explain why you will be late and ask for an extension of time. Check your contract to see if there are any penalites for late delivery.

16. MY PUBLISHER HAS MADE SOME EDITORIAL CHANGES, DO I HAVE TO ACCEPT THEM?

Yes, if your contract has a statement similar to this. "The Publisher may make such editorial changes in the manuscript as it deems necessary or advisable."

In any case, your publisher should be willing to consult you about any proposed changes and you should be willing to listen to him. A publisher usually has a valid reason for proposing changes.

17. I WANT TO USE A PSEUDONYM, HOW DOES THAT AFFECT MY CONTRACT?

Your contract will have to be signed under your legal name. Your publisher should be consulted on why you want to use a name other than your real name.

The name you write under should be one that you can live with for a long time. If you expect to write more than one book, you want to establish your reputation as a writer under that name.

It may not, strictly speaking, be a pseudonym that you choose. It may be a shortened form of your legal name. Some married women prefer to write under their maiden name or the name by which they became known even though they may have subsequently married two or more times.

Other writers feel that their real names are too long or too difficult to pronounce so they take a pen name. One writer, I know, took a family name as her pseudonym because she wanted to honor a dead relative. A poet uses a pen name for his poetry because he is well-known as a technical writer and wants to keep those two areas of his writing career separate.

18. WHO FURNISHES THE INDEX AND BIBLIOGRAPHY IF THEY ARE REQUESTED?

Your contract should specify this under the heading "Supplementary Materials" and should also denote a time limit for these to be done if you have to do them. If you are writing a non-fiction book which has required research you will already have a bibliography which should be included in your book.

The publisher may have a certain style for the bibliography which you must follow. If not, you can use the form recommended by any good style manual. The most important thing is to be consistant in how you make your entries.

Indexing is most often done by a professional indexer. Some publishers have persons on their staff who can index. There are also, especially in cities, freelance indexers. The public library or college library is a good place to get information about indexers in your area.

It should be understood in advance who, you or the publisher, is to pay for the indexing.

This is not to say that you can't provide your own index but it requires time and some skill. There are books available which will tell you how to index. Your decision about doing it yourself or having someone else do it will depend upon the complexity of the index.

19. WHEN SHOULD I EXPECT MY ROYALTIES?

Most standard contracts provide that statements of accounts will be made every six months. This is not six months after the signing of the contract but six months after the publication of the book and every six-month interval after that as long as the book is in print.

20. WHAT IS THE "OPTION" CLAUSE?

The option clause means that the publisher has the right of first refusal on your next book. It provides for negotiation of terms and has a time limit for acceptance or refusal.

COMPUTERS — YES OR NO?

1. **SHOULD I USE A COMPUTER/WORD PROCESSOR IN MY WRITING?**

   Saying yes or no to a computer is basically a personal decision. Do you feel comfortable using a typewriter? If you do then you will probably feel right at home transferring that skill to a computer.
   Would you use your computer enough to justify the initial expense and the subsequent upkeep?
   Don't mistake getting and using a computer with achieving success as a writer. A computer can make it easier for you to write but the ideas still have to come from you.

2. **HOW CAN A COMPUTER/WORD PROCESSOR HELP ME IN WRITING?**

   It will save you time. With a word processor it is easy to self-edit. You can make corrections, rearrange whole paragraphs, etc. with a single touch. Revision is simple and easy.

3. **DO I HAVE TO GET A BIG COMPUTER TO DO THIS?**

   No, the new small personal computers are very suitable for an individual's needs.

4. **HOW DO I KNOW WHICH COMPUTER TO BUY?**

   Don't be in a hurry! Shop around. Try several out and read the literature. Ask people who have computers what they like or dislike about their computers. There are now computer stores where you can examine various computers and other equipment, literature and software all in one place.

5. **WHAT DOES "HARDWARE" MEAN?**

   Hardware is the computer or machine.

6. **WHAT DOES "SOFTWARE" MEAN?**

   Software is the term used to describe the computer programs you can purchase..

7. **WHAT IS A "FLOPPY DISK"?**

   A magnetic disk which contains the information you put into the computer. It is your memory retention system.

8. **WHAT IS "DOCUMENTATION"?**

The manuals and other training devices that tell you how to use your computer and its programs. If you don't understand the documentation of a particular product, look for one that you can understand.

9. **WHAT IS "RAM"?**

RAM stands for random access memory, that is the memory capacity of your computer. The more complicated your program, the more memory capacity is needed. When you buy a program, check to see if the RAM required can be supplied by your computer. Your computer should have at least 64k of RAM (about 65,000 characters) to handle most word-processing programs.

10. **AM I GOING TO HAVE TO LEARN A WHOLE NEW LANGUAGE TO USE A COMPUTER?**

No, but you will have to learn a new vocabulary and new meanings for some familiar words such as "software" and "hardware". There is a continuing development in computer science to make the personal computers easy for the average person to use. This concept extends to the various computer components such as the programs. In fact, it is common to hear companies extol their computers as being "user-friendly" and certainly you will want to get a computer that you can understand and that will be able to understand you.

11. **WHAT DO I NEED IN ADDITION TO A COMPUTER AND APPROPRIATE SOFTWARE?**

You need a good quality printer. Printers come in either daisywheel or dot matrix. Daisywheel copy looks like typewritten copy but costs more than dot matrix which is a pattern of dots that the eye reads as letters. Dot matrix printers can also produce charts and drawings, daisywheels can't.

12. **WHAT SHOULD I LOOK FOR IN A PRINTER?**

First, be sure it will work (be compatible) with your computer. Second, check the printing quality. Are all the letters readable? The printer should also have a paper-advancing mechanism.

Check the noise level. Some printers are very noisy, others not much noisier than a typewriter. Think of where you are going to use it and when. A noisy printer in a small room can be very upsetting. Using a noisy printer late at night may cause family problems.

13. **WHAT OTHER THINGS DO I NEED TO BE AWARE OF BEFORE I GET MY COMPUTER?**

Find out if needed supplies are available locally and how much they will cost. Your computer will need various software packages; your printer will need ribbons and paper.

Is repair service readily available? Can someone answer your questions if a problem develops?

14. WILL PUBLISHERS ACCEPT COMPUTER PRINTOUTS?

Yes, most publishers do. Check your market listings, however, as they indicate which ones will accept computer printouts. Some publishers will specify that they prefer letter quality to dot matrix. An increasing number of publishers are willing to accept disk submissions.

15. CAN MY COMPUTER DO OTHER THINGS FOR ME?

Yes, with the right software packages you can use your computer to handle your budget, build your own reference programs and, if you have time, play games. The computer is limited only by what you put in to it.

BIBLIOGRAPHY

American Heritage Dictionary. Rev.ed. New York: Dell, 1983.

Association of American Publishers. *An Author's Primer to Word Processing.* New York: AAP, 1983.

Baker, George. *Dramatic Technique.* Philadelphia, PA: R. West, 1975.

Bartlett, John. *Familiar Quotations.* Secaucus, NJ: Lyle Stuart, 1983.

Beil, Norman. *The Writer's Legal and Business Guide: To Motion Pictures, Television and Book Publishing.* New York: Arco, 1984

Belkin, Gary S. *Getting Published: A Guide for Business People and Other Professionals.* New York: Wiley, 1984.

Block, Lawrence. *Writing the Novel: From Plot to Print.* Cincinnati, OH: Writer's Digest Books, 1979.

Brady, Ben. *The Keys To Writing for Television & Films.* 4th ed. Dubuque, IA: Kendall-Hunt, 1982.

Brady, John. *The Craft of Interviewing.* Cincinnati, OH: Writer's Digest Books, 1975.

Bunnin, Brad and Beren, Peter. *Author Law & Strategies.* Occidental, CA: Nolo Press, 1983.

Burack, Sylvia K. *The Writer's Handbook.* Boston, MA: The Writer, 1984.

_____. *Writing and Selling Fillers, Light Verse and Short Humor.* Boston, MA: The Writer, 1982.

_____. *Writing and Selling the Romance Novel.* Boston, MA: The Writer, 1983.

Burgett, Gordon. *How to Sell Seventy-Five Per Cent of Your Freelance Writing.* Carpinteria, CA: Write To Sell, 1983.

Capossela, Jim. *How To Write For the Sporting Magazines: A Concise Guide To Writing Fishing, Hunting & Other Outdoor Articles.* Tarrytown, NY: Northeast Sportsman, 1983.

Cassill, Kay. *The Complete Handbook for Freelance Writers.* Cincinnati, OH: Writer's Digest Books, 1981.

Cheney, Theodore A.R. *Getting the Words Right: How To Revise, Edit and Rewrite.* Cincinnati, OH: Writer's Digest Books, 1983.

Clark, Bernadine. *Writer's Resource Guide.* 2nd ed. Cincinnati, OH: Writer's Digest Books, 1983.

Cousin, Michelle. *Writing a Television Play.* Boston, MA: The Writer, 1975.

D'Ignazio, Fred. *How To Get Intimate With Your Computer: A Ten-Step Program for Relieving Computer Anxiety.* New York: McGraw-Hill, 1984.

Duncan, Lois. *How To Write and Sell Your Personal Experiences.* Cincinnati, OH: Writer's Digest Books, 1979.

Dymond, David. *Writing Local History: A Practical Guide.* Brookfield, VT: Brookfield Pub. Co., 1981.

Easton, Anthony T. *The Under $800 Computer Buyer's Guide: Evaluating the New Generation of Small Computers.* Reading, MA: Addison-Wesley, 1984.

Emmison, F.G. *Archives & Local History.* 2nd ed. Totowa, NJ: Rowman, 1974.

Freedman, Helen Rosengren and Krieger, Karen. *The Writer's Guide To Magazine Markets: Nonfiction.* New York, New American Library, 1983.

Gadney, Alan. *Busy Person's Guide To Selecting the Right Word Processor: A Visual Shortcut to Understanding and Buying.* Glendale, CA: Festival Pub., 1984.

_____. *How To Enter and Win Fiction-Writing Contests.* New York: Facts on File, 1981.

Glossbrenner, Alfred. *How To Buy Software: The Master Guide To Picking The Program.* New York: St. Martin's Press, 1984.

Helms, Harry. *The McGraw-Hill Computer Handbook.* New York: McGraw-Hill, 1983.

Herr, Ethel. *An Introduction To Christian Writing.* Wheaton, IL: Tyndale, 1983.

Hillyer, Robert. *First Principles of Verse.* Boston, MA: The Writer, 1950.

Holmes, Marjorie. *Writing the Creative Article.* Rev.ed. Boston, MA: The Writer, 1976.

Hoskins, W.G. *Fieldwork In Local History.* 2nd ed. Winchester, MA: Faber & Faber, 1982.

Hull, Raymond. *How To Write a Play.* Cincinnati, OH: Writer's Digest Books, 1983.

_____. *How To Write "How-To" Books and Articles.* Cincinnati, OH: Writer's Digest Books, 1981.

Jacobs, Hayes B. *Writing and Selling Non-Fiction.* Cincinnati, OH: Writer's Digest Books, 1975.

Jerome, Judson. *The Poet's Handbook.* Cincinnati, OH: Writer's Digest Books, 1980.

Kolve, Carolee Nance. *How To Buy (and Survive!) Your First Computer.* New York: McGraw-Hill/Byte, 1983.

Krieger, Karen and Freedman, Helen R. *The Writer's Guide To Magazine Markets: Fiction.* New York: NAL/Plume, 1983.

Literary Market Place, The Dictionary of American Book Publishing. New York: Bowker (an annual publication)

Lounsbury, Warren C. *Theatre Backstage from A—Z.* Rev.ed. Seattle, WA: University of Washington Press, 1972.

Lowery, Marilyn M. *How To Write Romance Novels That Sell.* New York: Rawson Wade, 1983.

Mack, Karin and Skjei, Eric. *Overcoming Writing Blocks.* Los Angeles, CA: J.P. Tarcher, 1979.

Marston, Doric Ricker. *A Guide To Writing History.* Cincinnati, OH: Writer's Digest Books, 1975.

Mystery Writers of America. *Mystery Writer's Handbook.* Cincinnati, OH: Writer's Digest Books, 1982.

Nash, Constance and Oakey, Virginia. *The Screenwriter's Handbook: What To Write, How To Write It, Where To Sell It.* New York: Barnes & Noble, 1978.

————. and ————. *The Television Writer's Handbook: What To Write, How To Write It, Where To Sell It.* New York: Barnes & Noble, 1978.

Norwick, Kenneth P. (and Others) *The Rights of Authors and Artists: The Basic ACLU Guide To the Legal Rights of Authors and Artists.* New York: Bantam, 1984.

Polking, Kirk and Meranus, Leonard S. *Law and the Writer.* Rev.ed. Cincinnati, OH: Writer's Digest Books, 1981.

Poynter, Dan. *Computer Selection Guide: Choosing the Right Hardware and Software: Business - Professional - Personal.* Santa Barbara, CA: Para, 1983.

Preston, Elizabeth. *A Writer's Guide To Copyright.* Boston, MA: The Writer, 1982.

Reader's Digest Editors. *Success With Words, a Guide To The American Language.* Pleasantville, NY: Reader's Digest Assoc., 1983.

Roberts, Ellen E.M. *The Children's Picture Book: How To Write It, How To Sell It.* Cincinnati, OH: Writer's Digest Books, 1981.

Rock, Maxine. *Fiction Writer's Help Book.* Cincinnati, OH: Writer's Digest Books, 1982.

Rodwell, Peter. *The Personal Computer Handbook.* Woodbury, NY: Barron's, 1983.

Rosenbaum, Jean & Rosenbaum Veryl. *The Writer's Survival Guide.* Cincinnati, OH: Writer's Digest Books, 1982.

Samson, Jack. *Successful Outdoor Writing.* Cincinnati, OH: Writer's Digest Books, 1979.

Science Ficiton Writers of America. *Writing and Selling Science Fiction.* Cincinnati, OH: Writer's Digest Books, 1982.

Shimberg, Elaine Fantle. *How To Be a Successful Housewife/Writer.* Cincinnati, OH: Writer's Digest Books, 1979.

Sitton, Thad (and Others). *Oral History: A Guide for Teachers and Others.* Austin: University of Texas, 1983.

Stern, Fred. *Word Processing and Beyond: the Introductory Computer Book.* Santa Fe, NM: John Muir, 1983.

Stevenson, John. *Writing Commercial Fiction.* Englewood Cliffs, NJ: Prentice-Hall, 1983.

Straczynski, J. Michael. *The Complete Book of Scriptwriting.* Cincinnati, OH: Writer's Digest Books, 1982.

Webster's New World Dictionary of Computer Terms. New York: Simon & Schuster, 1983.

Whitman, Ruth. *Becoming a Poet.* Boston, MA: The Writer, 1982.

Whitney, Phyllis A. *Guide To Fiction Writing.* Boston, MA: the Writer, 1982.

————. *Writing Juvenile Stories and Novels.* Boston, MA: the Writer, 1976.

The World Almanac & Book of Facts. New York: Newspaper Enterprise Association. (an annual publication)

Writer's Market: Where To Sell What You Write. Cincinnati, OH: Writer's Digest Books. (an annual publication)

Yolen, Jane. *Writing Books for Children.* Rev.ed. Boston, MA: The Writer, 1983.

Zobel, Louise Purwin. *The Travel Writer's Handbook.* Cincinnati, OH: Writer's Digest Books, 1980.